TRUMP

THE BLUE-COLLAR PRESIDENT

TRUMP

THE BLUE-COLLAR PRESIDENT

ANTHONY SCARAMUCCI

CENTER
STREET
New York Nashville

Center Street
Hachette Book Group
1290 Avenue of the Americas, New York, NY 10104
centerstreet.com
twitter.com/centerstreet

First Edition: October 2018

Center Street is a division of Hachette Book Group, Inc. The Center Street name and logo are trademarks of Hachette Book Group, Inc.

The publisher is not responsible for websites (or their content) that are not owned by the publisher.

The Hachette Speakers Bureau provides a wide range of authors for speaking events. To find out more, go to www.HachetteSpeakersBureau.com or call (866) 376-6591.

Library of Congress Cataloging-in-Publication Data has been applied for.

ISBNs: 978-1-5460-7592-9 (hardcover), 978-1-5460-7642-1 (signed edition), 978-1-5460-7640-7 (B&N signed edition), 978-1-5460-8198-2 (ebook)

Printed in the United States of America

LSC-C

10 9 8 7 6 5 4 3 2 1

For my wife, Deidre, thanks for sticking with me through a rough time. I love you more every day.

CONTENTS

CONTENTS

TRUMP

THE BLUE-COLLAR PRESIDENT

CHAPTER ONE

THE BILLIONAIRE BLUE-COLLAR PRESIDENT

Donald J. Trump, the president for the working class. (Saul Loeb AFP / Getty Images)

THE DAY AFTER President Trump appointed me to the job as White House communications director, *Long Island Newsday*, the newspaper I'd delivered as a kid, ran the story with my photograph on the front page. My eighty-year-old mother, who still lives with my dad in the house that I grew up in, bought a dozen copies at Jack's Stationery down on Main Street. She might have been more excited than I was. My brother, David, joked that she was going to take down the photos of all her grandchildren and replace them with the framed front page.

Eleven days later—and it was eleven days, not ten as widely reported (I'm not gonna let the media steal almost ten percent of my White House experience!)—after I'd been fired from the job because of an embarrassing public blowout with a reporter from the *New Yorker*, things weren't quite as heartwarming at the Scaramucci residence. The press descended like wasps on my parents' house. When I heard, I went over to see how my folks were doing. As I pulled into the driveway, my mother was standing in the front doorway as reporters pointed microphones and cameras at her. My mom had a look on her face that I knew well. It was the same expression she wore when she'd say to me, "Wait until your father gets home!"

"Get the f**k off my lawn!" she yelled at them.

"Ma," I said, "that's what got me in trouble in the first place."

★ / ★ / ★

MY BROTHER WAS ONLY half kidding about my mother taking down the photos of her grandchildren. The living room wall of my parents' house is made of that old-school 1970s paneling. It's right out of *The Brady Bunch*. It's also the Anthony Scaramucci "Wall of Fame." There are snapshots from high school to law school and everything in between, articles about my first two hedge funds, magazine profiles written well before "the Mooch" became a household name. Italian mothers can go overboard when it comes to two things: plastic-covered furniture and telling you how great their kids are. (My grandmother, my mom's mom, who lived just a block from us in Port Washington, actually did have plastic-covered furniture, as well as plastic-covered rugs in the hallways and plastic-covered lampshades.) Then, in a blink, I went from the "eighty-fifth most important person in global finance," according to *Worth* magazine, to off that list and into the abyss of political purgatory.

Still, modesty aside, Mom's homage to me sums up a pretty unlikely life, although one that began in an average way. I was born in a small working-class enclave of Long Island, where my father started out with an hourly wage measuring the sand that was poured into barges and shoveling sand and stone from the ground. My mother stayed home and raised her children. I went to college and then a fancy law school on loans and a little cash from my father's life insurance policy and savings. I followed my older brother to Wall Street, where I immediately got fired from Goldman Sachs, failed the bar exam twice, and was rehired at Goldman, all in about a year. From there on, however, my life went straight up like a rocket. I passed the bar, started a family and two successful companies, witnessed firsthand 9/11, survived the financial crisis, threw a legendary hedge fund conference called SALT in Las Vegas nine years in a row, twice in Singapore, and once in Tokyo, and had my own finance show on television. After all that, I backed my way into presidential politics the way most people get into drugs.

Along the way, I made friends with a billionaire real estate developer from Manhattan, a man who would go on to become the forty-fifth president of the United States. I was among the first people to learn Donald Trump was running for president (although I didn't believe him at the time), and we ran in the same circles and attended the same charity and political fund-raisers. For a short time, I was even a political antagonist who challenged him to fights on television. Somehow, all that earned me a spot on the political campaign of the century, raising money and stumping for the candidate on TV. It was Donald Trump himself who ultimately gave me my eleven days of fame in the White House; and it was Donald Trump who had to toss me out, like an empty Big Mac box, when the time came.

In one way, this book is the story of my life and my unique friendship with the president, but in the larger view, it's also the story of an America that changed dramatically during those years.

Both Donald Trump and I had fathers who thrived in the prosperity of the postwar years and benefited from America's firm belief and investment in its middle and lower classes. One father dug the sand that made cement, and the other poured the cement into the foundation on which the American Dream was built. The America they grew up in was founded on a solid economic footing; it was unafraid to assert itself on the world stage when necessary. As we, their sons, came along, and the twentieth century wore on, some of that prosperity vanished before our eyes. The trade deals we had struck in the aftermath of the war became worse and worse as they were renegotiated by elitist politicians out of touch with the American worker, and our tax system fell far out of balance with what was sensible and necessary. The American government then laid the groundwork for a financial collapse and blamed its most influential financial institutions when that collapse happened. Our leaders became feckless and unable to stand up for the United States of America. The aspirational working class—hardworking men and women who, like Fred Trump and Alexander Scaramucci, had struggled to achieve success—suffered a sharp decline while career politicians in Washington lined their pockets and held Congress in gridlock. With the coming of the internet, vast, powerful companies run by tech oligarchs controlled the content we read and the things we bought. Though these companies professed to be progressive, their actions were actually intrusive, racist, and limiting.

The lives of American citizens declined too, and when those people looked for help, no one was listening. At least not until the most improbable of all candidates came riding out of New York to champion their cause.

FOR MY MONEY, however, the best stories are comeback stories. You know the moment in *Rocky* when the music starts to swell and Balboa is getting up from the mat? It's when Apollo Creed starts looking worried, and the camera zooms in for a tight shot of Rocky's puffy "Cut me, Mick" eye. If you're like me, that's when you start getting butterflies. That's when the story really begins to mean something to you—maybe because, like me, you've been down on the mat yourself. You know what it feels like to be counted out and to know at the same time, with absolute certainty, that you haven't thrown your last punch.

While I was making my way through the Ivy League and the upper crust of New York finance, Donald Trump was down in construction sites with his contractors, slipping hundred-dollar bills to waiters in the restaurants on his properties, and fixing up an ice

6

rink in New York City when the government got too bloated and arrogant to do the job. He would also become one of the greatest brand-builders and businessmen of our time. He existed in a world of stratospheric wealth, and yet somehow was able to hold onto the blue-collar world of his father all at once.

I, on the other hand, let wealth and influence change me. The more I made, the further I descended into the echo chamber of private clubs and wealthy communities until I forgot all about the sand my father dug. It embarrasses me to admit this, but I so wanted to move into the world of financial independence that I slowly became ignorant of the blue-collar struggle that began to surround me.

Then came May of 2016, and a Trump rally in Albuquerque. It was the first event I'd attended as a member of the Donald J. Trump for President campaign. I walked through the crowd that had gathered by the thousands outside a convention center. I listened to story after story of economic strife and pain. I don't remember if it was after the third or the thirteenth version of the same story when the epiphany happened. All I know is that it did.

Though I was in Albuquerque and the accent was different, I might as well have been in Port Washington on Long Island. The block I grew up on had landscapers, telephone linemen, cops, nurses, and firefighters. My father lost most of his hearing from the blasting at his job. We were the definition of blue collar, and our neighborhood had once made anything seem possible. So too had neighborhoods in Scranton, Beaumont, Santa Fe, and hundreds of other places across the country. We had gone from aspirational neighborhoods to desperational ones.

Those neighborhoods had been victimized by decades of unfair trade policy and anti-working-class legislation, and I, soaring far above the problems on the ground, had paid little attention to them. It took the campaign of a guy who lived in a tower on Fifth Avenue next to Tiffany to show me what was happening to America's working class.

In the pages ahead, I'll also show you how Donald Trump is changing that. I'll deconstruct the beginnings of Trumponomics from an insider's point of view, tracing the economic and cultural forces that have made it necessary. I'll show you how his economic policies came about and how they will work for you. I'll do the same with Donald Trump's foreign and domestic policy achievements, place them into a historical framework, and look ahead to what they may bring in the future. I've always thought of myself as a guy who calls balls and strikes as I see them, however, and this book will be no different. Where I have problems with President Trump's agenda, or think he made missteps, I'll say so. And though my missteps could fill a phone book, here you'll get the *Reader's Digest* "abridged version."

THERE'S ONE MORE thing I discuss in the pages ahead, but for the life of me, I can't remember what it is...Oh yeah! The old elephant in the room! So if you picked up this book hoping to find out the inside story of my time in, and sudden departure from, the West Wing, don't worry; I won't disappoint you. Though short, those days were some of the Trump administration's most tumultuous and formative, and I will reveal the stories behind the headlines and expose those responsible for much of the administration's early discord. I hold nothing back (except the profanity), and spare no one, especially myself.

Still, I'll tell you the same thing I tell everyone who asks about my eleven days in the White House: it was the twelfth day that mattered. That was the day I got up off the mat again, just like this great country of ours is in the process of doing.

As I sat in my parents' living room that day, the mailbox on my cell phone filled with messages from reporters. Most of them were probably hoping I would trash the president for firing me, lacing my speech with four-letter words, just as I had done on the phone call with the *New Yorker* writer (more on that later). Wasn't going to happen. First of all, I hold no anger toward the president. I'd given him little choice. Second of all, if I learned one thing about talking with reporters, it's that most of them would double-cross their mothers for a story that goes viral. I should have known that before I started in the White House, you're probably thinking to yourself, and you're right.

It was as I looked again at the story of my life on the living room wall that the idea of this book began to form. In the days that followed, I went out to California to see my oldest son, AJ. I made a few appearances on television and the radio, including a tough interview on *The Late Show with Stephen Colbert* and a fun podcast with the guys from *Barstool Sports*. I answered every question they asked as honestly as I could. I told them the real story. I didn't, however, have the chance to tell the whole story.

That is, until now.

CHAPTER TWO

THE GREAT AMERICA

"Do not let anyone tell you it cannot be done. No challenge can match the heart and fight and spirit of America."

President DONALD J. TRUMP
inaugural address, January 20, 2017

I MAGINE, IF YOU will, that you're watching a movie in reverse. My hair goes from its current "Latin American dictator brown" (I tried to dye it "Cuban leader midnight," but it looked terrible on TV) to *Saturday Night Fever* black, and then back to a fifth-grade buzz cut. Now I'm in the crib. Then my mom's pregnant with me. Now she's a little girl. The skyscrapers in New York are coming down; the Brooklyn Bridge recedes. Roads turn to dirt and then grass. There go Ronald Reagan, Sam Rayburn, Teddy Roosevelt.

Andrew Jackson. Some cavemen.

A bear.

We can stop there: three million years ago.

It's about 2,700,000 BCE, and the Catskill Mountains, which will become little sissy hills in a few years, are taller than the Himalayas. Their peaks reach about thirty thousand feet above sea level, and they're wider than most US states. Inside are massive deposits of limestone, sandstone, and shale. Some of the toughest, most malleable material on earth. Wooly mammoths run over the peaks. Primitive versions of the vampire bat—a distant ancestor of Steve Bannon, I believe—hang upside down in the caves. There's a glacier coming from up north, near what's now New England. It's massive and moving, at least by glacial standards, pretty quickly.

A few million years go by.

This glacier sweeps over the East Coast like some giant earthmover and demolishes the Catskill Mountains. Under the ice, all that sediment and rich material that made up the mountains gets broken up and frozen, then gobbled up into the glacial mass. It moves south as the edge of the glacier creeps down the coast until it covers most of the continent.

Then, in 9,000 BCE, the glacier gets stuck. It stops moving at the mouth of a dried-up riverbed near what's now eastern New York. There it starts to melt at the same rate it advances. Meaning: the thing sits there and melts. For a few thousand years, getting ever smaller, the glacier sits at the edge of the sea and dumps millions of tons of rock, gravel, and sand into the ocean. Before long there's a big, long pile of sediment and thick, gravelly sand—the largest sandbank east of the Mississippi.

Long Island.

My home.

★ ∕ ★ ∕ ★

WHEN MY PATERNAL grandfather, Alessandro Scaramucci, first came to the United States in the 1890s, he blew right past Long Island. He and his brothers had been coal miners in Campagna, Italy. When they heard that they could get good work mining coal in the hills of northeastern Pennsylvania, they dropped their picks and sailed.

What they heard was right. There was coal in the Pennsylvania hills. Plenty of it.

My grandfather and his wife moved west and settled in a small mining town called Plains near Scranton, Pennsylvania. There they mined for anthracite coal during the day and slept in a narrow split-level house at night. The coal they mined went to power multicycle engines, heat houses, and produce electricity for most of America east of the Mississippi. It was good work if you didn't mind the occasional mine collapse and black lung, and, thanks to the union, it paid a decent wage.

Alessandro, however, hated it. The mines were dark and confined; the air was thick with dust. After a few years of working down in the mines, he quit to open a grocery store. He was more comfortable selling food and supplies to the miners than he was climbing down into the hole with them. In the store, he'd chop meat and work behind the counter as a butcher. In a hardworking town like Scranton, good meat was a luxury. Business was steady for a while.

He and my grandmother had seven children. My father, Alexander, was the youngest. All nine of them lived in a house built for three. One of the reasons I never complained about my upbringing, apart from simple respect for my parents, was that I used to hear my father's stories about the house in Plains, with its single bathroom and tiny beds split between brothers. Today Zillow lists the house for $43,000. You can imagine what it cost eighty years ago. The house I grew up in was Mar-a-Lago in comparison.

Though coal was king in the early part of the twentieth century, the crown started to slip after World War I. Decreased demand due to alternative fuels, mostly petroleum products, and labor strikes sounded the death knell for coal. Then came the Depression, and coal country was laid to waste. Though there was a slight resurgence during World War II, VE and VJ Day signaled not the coming of the prosperous years most of the county would enjoy, but more despair. Like the Trump rallies during the presidential campaign, coal country was filled with the forgotten Americans. Even when the pages of the *New York Times* told them things were great—the stock market is on an upswing, the job numbers are high, we've got better quality-of-life numbers than ever—people in places like northeastern Pennsylvania felt left behind. No one was listening to them.

I N THE MONTHS after World War II, with the stock market streaking to heights no one had ever imagined possible and the soldiers coming home in droves, both American coasts were alive with celebration. Ticker tape rained from the skies. In Washington, politicians were busy drafting an agreement that would raise Europe from the rubble of the war and help them sustain themselves economically. Significant parts of that continent were in ruins, and politicians feared rapid inflation.

Faced with the decision of whether to let the countries suffer and collapse or to prop them up and establish an international coalition to ensure peace, Congress and the Truman administration chose the latter. It was the right decision. The Marshall Plan, named after Secretary of State George C. Marshall, a retired five-star general who first proposed the plan in a speech at Harvard, gave billions of dollars of aid to struggling European economies. It enabled them to rebuild the roads and bridges that had been destroyed by invasions and bombs, and it gave wary farmers and business owners a kind of assurance that it was safe to get back into the market. More than anything, the Marshall Plan provided these countries security—an assurance that the United States of America would not let them fail. We even accepted an uneven playing field to help them rebuild and grow.

While the Marshall Plan was a good idea for the short term, it would have devastating consequences on the American worker for decades to come. Allow me to explain.

What had to happen for the Marshall Plan to be successful—for the world to be sure it'd seen the last of these all-encompassing wars for a long, long time—was a slight tipping of trade policy in favor of all countries other than the United States. The plan sent billions

of dollars of aid to countries like Germany, France, and England—
countries that were trying to establish their own mills and factories so they could compete in the global market. This came at the
expense of investment in American factories, and laid the groundwork for decades of unfair trade policy.

Here's an analogy. Imagine there was a baseball league and
you had one team with ten of the best players who'd ever played
the game—guys like Mickey Mantle, Keith Hernandez, Johnny
Bench—and there were another five or six teams filled with minor
leaguers and rookies. It wouldn't be fair, right? The games wouldn't
be fun to watch, and if the lesser teams were spending their whole
season getting beat up on, the rookies wouldn't get any better. This
was the situation between the United States and Europe in the
aftermath of World War II. Our continent hadn't seen any fighting,
and our factories had been steadily producing for the war effort. We
had a team of all-stars.

So, we took cash we could have invested in our own infrastructure and development and gifted it to European countries so that
they could build a robust world economy. As you probably know,
there was also a significant upside for the United States. European
economies provided a huge new market for American goods and
allowed us to produce more than we ever had before.

All through the twentieth century, we would continue to make
trade policy this way. Our relationships with other countries—our
allies in particular—were always built on a framework of benevo-
lence and charity, made under the presumption that healthy competition was a good thing.

In the years immediately following the war, European countries
built up remarkable manufacturing infrastructures of their own,
allowing the gross national products of Marshall Plan countries
to grow as much as 25 percent by the end of the 1940s. While the

United States wouldn't begin feeling the harsh effects of these uneven trade deals for a few decades—right around the time we started to hear words like "tariffs," "steel," and "Donald Trump" on the news—there were more immediate consequences too. And most of the burden, as it often does, fell on the working class. (We'll talk more about this later in the book.)

In the aftermath of the war, towns like Plains saw an influx of uneven competition and the sharp decline of its manufacturing sector. The mills were closing, and the mines were being shuttered. The line for jobs was long. After he had to close his shop, my grandfather took a job as a janitor in a school miles away from home. Every morning, he put on a uniform instead of his butcher's apron and cleaned up after kids younger than his own. He died of a heart attack before he turned seventy-one.

Alexander Scaramucci, my dad, knew little of the balance of the world's economy and its effect on places like northeastern Pennsylvania. All he knew was that the future didn't look friendly. If he stuck around Plains he would have a long life working the coal mines or, worse, no work at all, to look forward to. All around him were poverty and despair. In 1953 he wrote to his brother, Orlando Scaramucci, for help.

Orlando, twelve years older than my father, had joined the army during World War II and ended up in Italy battling the Germans. There he met a young nurse named Jeane. She was a slight woman with soft hands and a nice smile. With the horror of war surrounding them, they fell in love. When the war ended, they moved back to her hometown, a quaint little village called Port Washington on Long Island. They were married in St. Peter's Church in town. Orlando took a job with Jeane's father at a company called Gotham Sand and Stone.

Orlando wrote back to my dad and told him to come to Port

Washington. The ocean was near, and there was sand enough to dig for lifetimes.

My father headed east right after high school and moved in with his brother. He started to work in the sandpits on the stone dock right after he arrived, making the same motions and building the same muscles his grandfather and father had in the coal mines. But he did it in the open air of Long Island—air that was free of coal dust and scented with salt from the sea.

The town of Port Washington sits on a five-square-mile peninsula jutting into the Long Island Sound, just seventeen miles east of Manhattan. The town is named after our first president, who was quartered there during the Revolutionary War. The area is rich in the history of our fight for independence. Many of the streets are named after the Founders. Off the northern tip of the peninsula, in the Long Island Sound, is a small island called Execution Rocks. A lighthouse stands on the island now, but during the Revolution British troops would chain colonial captives to the rocky shore of the island at low tide and let them die slowly as the waters rose.

It was not out in the Sound, however, but onshore where this story continues. Unlike beach sand, Gotham's sand was coarse, and it mixed perfectly with cement. Once it was mined, the sand was moved by conveyor belt onto barges in the Long Island Sound, and then tugged by boat to Long Island City. There workers in factories would mix the sand with gravel, cement powder, and water, and then roll it around in big tumblers to make concrete. Trucks would then haul the concrete over the Queensboro Bridge.

Builders and contractors in Manhattan would watch the cement trucks come off the bridge like an endless caravan—the trucks carried some 140 million cubic yards of sand over the years.

The concrete in those trucks would become streets, sidewalks, and the most famous skyline in the world. The Empire State

Building, the Chrysler Building, and the Twin Towers of the World Trade Center were made from Gotham's sand.

A S THE CEMENT trucks first began to roll over the Queensboro Bridge, a young man named Frederick Trump, the first child of French and German immigrants who'd come to the United States in the late nineteenth century, began to pour his own concrete across the East River.

Fred Trump began his career building garages at the age of fifteen in Queens, where his family had settled after arriving in America. He graduated from garages to single-family homes that sold for $3,999. In 1939, taking advantage of a program offered by the Federal Housing Authority, which began giving home buyers low-interest, twenty-five-year mortgages, he nearly caused a stampede of home buyers. While building a new tract of homes in Coney Island, he parked his sixty-five-foot yacht with huge "Trump Show Boat" signs offshore. From the boat, he blasted patriotic music and released fish-shaped balloons, each carrying a coupon for either $25 or $250 toward a new Trump home. Now you know where his son Donald got it from.

During World War II, the elder Trump built barracks and apartments for the US Navy in Newport News and Norfolk, Virginia. After the war, he built long, low-slung apartment complexes and high-rise towers, set close together and built for as little money as possible. Many of them are still standing today.

Through the 1950s and '60s, Fred Trump watched the city change, and he adjusted his business model accordingly. Because of crime, overcrowding, and the fact that they were starting families, people began moving from the inner city to outer boroughs like

Queens, Brooklyn, and Staten Island. This was the beginning of the same exodus that would fill suburbs like mine in Long Island. Most of the men making this exodus were the sons of immigrants as Fred Trump was; many had just returned from the war, bought homes on the G.I. Bill, and found work in the city. The population of the outer boroughs ballooned, and civil service departments struggled to keep up.

It seemed there was nowhere left to live, and nowhere to build but up.

So Fred bought up more patches of land in Queens, and began building tall, thin apartment buildings. He put them up in small groupings of three and four along major train lines, using affordable materials when he could so the rents would be low. Between the buildings he planted grass and laid thin strips of concrete—most of which were made with that good old Port Washington sand—so the parks would take on the quality of a neighborhood. He knew that a good place to live is important to working people, and that a strong sense of community can change a person's life.

When his son Donald was home from military school in the '60s, Fred would often take him on walks around the complexes. They'd inspect buildings, check the status of repairs, and even collect rent from the tenants if they had the time.

One afternoon, they went to see a tenant who was a few months behind on his rent. In the apartment, the man explained that he had been laid off from his job, and there was no other source of income. In the apartment with him were his beleaguered-looking wife and three small children. In such a tight housing market, there were plenty of landlords who wouldn't think twice about throwing the family onto the street. Not Fred Trump. Instead, he and Donald sat for a while and talked with the family. They listened to the man tell them how he lost his job, and how he was out looking for a new one.

"Don't pay anything until you get back on your feet," Fred told him. "Even if it takes a few months."

When his son announced his run for president, the media would often try to make Fred Trump into a flagrant racist or some dictatorial landlord out of a Dickens novel. Donald Trump's father was no ballerina, and, like his son, was successful in a rough business. But the allegations leveled at him by the press weren't even remotely true. The media had become so blinded by their hatred for Donald Trump that they were even willing to print lies about a good man like his father—a man who was no longer alive to defend himself— to take him down.

But they couldn't take him down, at least not in the president's eyes. When Donald Trump talks of his dad there is a wistful reverence in his tone, one that makes it clear that he wants to emulate the kind of understanding and compassion his father had. Even today, beneath a tough exterior, it's there. I know because I've seen it.

Though Fred could be sympathetic, he was also known as being frugal. The president remembers walking into his father's office one day and seeing him struggling to put a broom together. It was cheaper to buy it in parts, he told his son. Fred would walk through construction sites picking up good nails and handing them back to the carpenters. Like father, like son. When he was running the Trump Organization, Donald Trump knew where all the nails were too.

The people who moved into Fred Trump's apartments were a lot like my parents, folks trying to improve their station in life by providing a nice home for their families. My father and Fred Trump lived by the simple American equation: the harder you worked, the more opportunity you afforded your family.

Theirs was an American story replicated millions and millions of times across our country. If the American Dream is an equation, with builders like Fred Trump at the beginning, banks and lending institutions in the middle, and homebuyers like my parents on the end, this was the time when everything added up.

Together, they built the Great America.

CHAPTER THREE

FROM SCHLEMIEL TO MENSCH

"Life is much more successfully looked at
from a single window."

—F. Scott Fitzgerald,
The Great Gatsby

Fred Trump, Sr., July 1965. (New York Daily News Archive / Getty Images)

THEY SAY THAT F. Scott Fitzgerald drew inspiration for his American classic when he lived across Manhasset Bay from Sands Point in Great Neck, New York. There he would attend parties at a house owned by a famous journalist named Herbert Bayard Swope. Swope's house sat on the Kings Point end of the Great Neck peninsula, and Fitzgerald would sit on the porch of the home with his drinking buddy, the writer Ring Lardner. Their boozy view was of Manhasset Bay and the lights on the docks of Sands Point, some of them, no doubt, green and barely visible to them just like the light on Daisy's dock was to Nick Carraway.

"I had a view of the water, a partial view of my neighbor's lawn, and the consoling proximity of millionaires," Fitzgerald wrote.

In Fitzgerald's day, it was the Hearsts, the Vanderbilts, and the Guggenheims who owned houses in Sands Point. Over the years, the names of the residents there have changed, and nearly all of the Gold Coast mansions are gone, but that strip of seaside land that Fitzgerald called East Egg in *The Great Gatsby* is still some of the priciest in the country.

★ ✦ ★ ✦ ★

THOUGH I LIVED only a couple of miles from Sands Point, the cost of the Scaramucci mansion on Webster Avenue in Port

Washington was a few commas short of its wealthy neighbors. It's not like we were poor. I would never disparage my father by saying that. We had macaroni on the table, wore Sears Toughskins jeans, and had air conditioners that went into the windows at the beginning of the summer, and out when the leaves started to fall.

But as a kid, I would ride my bike north on the Port Washington peninsula and down Middle Neck Road to Sands Point to look at the beautiful homes. In my day, people such as Averell Harriman and Perry Como owned them. As I'd pedal by, I'd dream that someday I was going to live in one of them. I dreamed the American Dream.

My father worked from seven o'clock in the morning until sundown. He and his brother would dig for the sand and limestone and shale that'd been dumped so many years before by that big glacial mass.

When he first came to Port Washington, Dad also moonlighted as a soda jerk at a diner called Freddy's. Though he'd work a second job for most of his early adult life, that first part-time gig was maybe his most important. It changed his life and also had a significant impact on mine.

One day, a couple of high school girls came into the diner. One of them was petite with dark hair and eyes and looked, as she would later often remind us and just about anyone else, like Natalie Wood. Alexander, who was only a couple of years older, struck up a conversation. The Natalie Wood look-alike, whose real name was Marie DeFeo, wanted to go to the beach with the friends who had come with her. Dad had a bucket-of-bolts old Chevy and offered them a ride. On the way, a tire on the Chevy went flat. As Dad was jacking up the car, my mother made a wise remark, one of a million she would deliver to him over the course of their marriage, and Alexander wiped his greasy hand on her shirt. Theirs was a romance just like Tony and Maria's in *West Side Story*. Well, sort of, if Tony and Maria argued all the time!

Mom and Dad were married in 1957 in St. Peter's, the same church as his brother Orlando, and for a few years lived in an apartment on Madison Street in Port Washington. A small pond, part of a park, sat in front of the apartment building. The town gave a contractor permission to drain the pond and fill it with soil so he could build a house on the lot. Each time my father walked out of the apartment in the morning heading for work, and at night when he'd come home, he'd stop for a moment and watch as the workers first poured the concrete for the foundation, then hammered together the frame, and finally built the roof and siding of the house on the corner of Webster Avenue and Madison Street. It was more than just curiosity that drew his gaze; it was his dream taking shape. Dad scraped together the five grand for the down payment and received a thirty-year mortgage for the other $11,000. The year was 1962.

Now, I'd like to say we were just like Ozzie and Harriet, but that would be a lie. The house was two stories, and my parents; my younger sister, Susan; brother, David; and I all slept in three small bedrooms on the second floor and shared one bathroom. That alone caused more friction than the Gaza Strip.

My parents mostly spoke Italian in the house, but wouldn't allow us to speak it at all. They wanted us to assimilate, they said, which was an excellent way of saying they didn't want us to know what they were talking about. There are some words for which you don't need a translator, however. The language in my house was loud and, well, colorful. That never changed. (Now you know where I got it from.) Though my dad wanted us to be thoroughly American, he had no problem teaching us old-world ways when it came to discipline. My brother, sister, or I would do something wrong, and my mother would say the words that I mentioned, the ones that sent a shiver through us: "Wait until your father gets home!" The worst thing that could happen was Dad coming through the door at 5:15 p.m., after working in the sandpits all day, and Mom lighting him up about something we had done. There was no question you were going to get your ass kicked. Dinner was at 5:15 sharp. My mother would have it on the table waiting for him. If one of us kids showed up at 5:16, watch out.

Though we had our fair share of dysfunction, we also had some fun.

Our house sat right next to Main Street School and its baseball field and playground. I was a pretty good athlete, a combination first baseman, point guard, and quarterback (until I got hurt in my junior year). I was also a big baseball fan, a long-suffering New York Mets fan. My uncle John took me to my first game at Shea Stadium when I was six. I remember it like it was yesterday, the grass as green as emeralds. I would read about my favorite players, such as Tom Seaver, Jon Matlack, and Rusty Staub, in the *New York Daily News* that my father brought home from work every day. Phil Pepe and Dick Young were my favorite sports columnists.

My father also taught me how to hunt and fish. Dad was a dedicated hunter, hard-core stuff. I'm not talking squirrel hunting with BB guns. We had a Winchester semiautomatic and a Remington 12-gauge shotgun in the house. Because of my dad, I'm a big proponent of the Second Amendment.

Dad belonged to the Arrowhead Hunting Club, an organization made up of Italian men. The club would spend hunting weekends in a small lodge in New York State near the Delaware Water Gap. When we were old enough, David and I would go along. We went every Thanksgiving weekend. These guys were real hunters. After they shot a deer, they would gut the animal, put it on the hood of their cars, and drive back to the lodge. There Dad and his friends would butcher it. I watched once, and never did again. Absolutely disgusting. That one time was enough to keep me out of a career as a surgeon. After they butchered the meat they'd freeze it, put it in a cooler, and then hand it out to the older Italian ladies back home in the neighborhood.

The best memory I have of back then, however, was breakfast. A couple of the men would get up at three thirty in the morning and make stacks of pancakes with mounds of butter and maple syrup tapped right from a tree. Tons of bacon and eggs. It was like they were short-order cooks at a diner.

Dad would also take us fishing. We would drive to the end of Long Island, and we would take one of the charter boats at Montauk. My brother always got seasick and would spend the whole trip in the hull of the boat. David and I fought a lot, and I always took a beating. When he was in the hull throwing up his guts into a bucket, I would smile at the thought that God was getting back at him for kicking my ass all the time. He also peed on my back in the bathtub when I was four. That son of a bitch! Some things you never forget.

THE OTHER THING all the Scaramucci kids did was work. My first real job was a paper route that I got when I was eleven. I was an entrepreneur from the start of my business career. I noticed that most of the *Newsday* paperboys would zip by the houses on their bikes and throw the papers onto the driveways, or would at least aim for the driveway. It was not unusual at all for the newspaper to end up in the bushes, under the customer's car, or even on the next-door neighbor's lawn. Although I had an arm better than most kids my age, I realized right away that the newspaper delivery business was a service industry. In any service industry, the first thing you have to do is take care of the customer.

I would park my Schwinn ten-speed at the base of the driveway, walk up to the door, and lay the paper flat on the porch. That was the Scaramucci Touch. I also took notice of all the houses that weren't getting a paper. For every house or apartment I delivered to, there were at least five that didn't subscribe to *Newsday*. In the business world we call that growth opportunity. I wanted to expand my customer base, and I thought I knew how I'd do it.

On Wednesdays, I would go to see Mr. Fusco, my boss at Long Island *Newsday*, and talk him into giving me thirty or so extra papers. Then I'd go to houses and buildings such as the Dolphin Green apartments near my house, and put my plan into action.

After I'd delivered to a regular customer, I'd knock on their neighbor's door and hand them a free paper.

I remember a woman named Mrs. Sheridan. When she answered the door, I said: "I'm Anthony Scaramucci, Marie's kid." (My mother knew everybody and everybody's business. She was Siri and Google before there were Siri and Google. You wanted to know who was having an affair in Port Washington, you went to see my mother.) "I noticed you haven't been taking the newspaper. I wanted to give you this free copy of *Long Island Newsday*, and see if you liked it."

Mrs. Sheridan took it, thanked me, and headed back inside. I wrote her name down in my red notebook—I kept meticulous notes, so I knew everyone who'd taken one of my papers—and then I went about making the rest of my deliveries. When I came around to collect money for the papers at the end of the week, I knocked on Mrs. Sheridan's door again.

"I hope you enjoyed the paper, Mrs. Sheridan," I said. "Could I put you down for daily delivery, weekend-only, or Sunday-only? *Newsday* would love to have you as a customer."

Mrs. Sheridan took the subscription and ended up being one of my best tippers. With the money I made from the route, I was able to take the Long Island Rail Road out to Shea Stadium to watch my beloved Mets play in person.

I quit the job only because I wanted to play baseball in high school. When I did, I had the largest paper route in the area. They had to hire four paperboys to take it over!

I N THE POSTWAR years, the population on Long Island tripled to 1.5 million people. Many of the families who moved into my neighborhood came from New York City's outer boroughs. Italians, Irish, Jews, cops, firefighters, garment workers, you name it, they came. Almost all of them had children and almost all of them were Democrats when they lived in New York City. They became Republicans as soon as they bought a lawn mower. For them, Long Island was where the American Dream lived, and the Republican Party was the keeper of that dream.

Traditionally, unions in America were aligned with the Democratic Party. Republicans were not perceived as friends of the working class. They were anti–New Deal, and authors of anti-labor-union legislation such as the Taft-Hartley Act and Landrum-Griffin Act, which restricted and regulated labor unions. But not in Nassau and Suffolk, Long Island's two counties. There, if you were in a private-sector union or part of a labor community, you were in the Grand Old Party. Not only were you Republican, you helped turn out the vote and campaigned for Republican candidates. It was said that Nassau and Suffolk turned out more Republican votes than any other two counties in the country. In turn, Republican-elected officials looked after the interests of the workers.

If you worked in the sandpits, like my dad, you were a Republican and you were a Margiotta man.

Joseph M. Margiotta, Joltin' Joe they called him, was the

chairman of the Nassau County Republican Party. What Boss Tweed was to Tammany Hall and New York City, Margiotta was to Nassau County and its Republicans. There were people in town who would call him before they called the police or the assigned government agency. He was in total control of county political appointments, patronage jobs, and seasonal workers. You wanted a job as a lifeguard at Jones Beach, but your parents were Democrats? You had a better chance of drowning in the ocean.

Along with getting a job for your nephew, Joe had other talents. Every May, he ran one of the most lucrative and influential political fund-raising dinners in the country. Along with the cash he collected that night—$2 million or more back in the day when $2 million meant something in politics—he also drew the biggest names in the Republican Party such as Richard Nixon and Ronald Reagan. Anybody who was anybody or wanted to be somebody bought a seat at Joe's dinner.

Every afternoon, I'd read stories about Joe and the guys he ran with in *Newsday*. The newspaper wasn't kind to him. No big shock there. In print, Margiotta's brand of politics seemed like a shady network of backstabbers and glad-handers, guys who'd smile to your face and then kick you in the nuts. I decided early on that I'd stay away from it.

I guess I should have written that down.

Still, one of the biggest thrills of my young life came when I was in high school, one that I believe set me on my conservative path, and Margiotta was responsible for it.

It happened like this: I went to Paul D. Schreiber High School in Port Washington. I'm proud to say I'm a product of a very good public school system. If you could take a time machine and go back, however, you'd see me in my burgundy Camaro, which my brother and I shared, tooling down Main Street, shirtless in the summer, chains around my neck, hair blown back; playing the radio (with power boosters on), listening to Led Zeppelin, Foreigner, or Billy Joel (singing "Anthony works at the grocery store / Savin' his pennies for someday"); doing fifty push-ups to pump up my chest in a disco parking lot; hanging out at the town dock with my friends; going to the Beacon Theater to see a movie on Saturday night; or working at Ghost Motorcycle with my cousins. (I'll tell you more about Ghost in a minute.) I wasn't a complete Guido, but I was close.

Schreiber High also held six or seven socials a year called bee-hives. The beehives were the impetus for my entrance into politics. The senior class president got to pick the films that we would show, was in charge of the soda machine revenue that went to funding the socials and, most importantly, got to pick the bands that played at the dances.

For my campaign, I played to my strengths: public speaking and networking. To be honest, though, the reason I won is because I ran against two girls who both happened to be Jewish and they ended up splitting the Jewish vote.

Along with orchestrating the socials, there was another perk I received as class president. Every year, Joe Margiotta would take kids in student governments in high schools across Long Island on a political field trip. That senior year, the trip was to the Plaza Hotel in New York City to meet Ronald Reagan. I wore a suit—100 percent polyester—and I had a pimple on my forehead. I remember the moment vividly not only because I got to meet one of the greatest American presidents, but because there were seven hundred thousand people in Manhattan protesting him for deploying nuclear weapons to Western Europe, and it seemed like most of them were right in front of the hotel.

This was June 1982. The *Daily News* had kept me apprised of Reagan's presidency, and just a year and a half into his first term, he'd already had quite a run. In March 1981, John Hinckley Jr. shot him in the chest in front of a Washington Hilton Hotel; the following July he had championed a 25 percent tax cut; in August he fired striking air traffic controllers; and in November his own budget director, David Stockman, would announce that Reagan's "supply side" economics benefited the rich more than anyone else. On top of all of that, he had about a million protesters following him around.

I was right next to Margiotta when he strode up to President Reagan—we were no more than two feet from the great man. Tall, with a mane of hair that seemed tinted red and a weathered face, he seemed to me almost unreal, an automated version out of a presidential exhibit in Disney World. I'd seen that famous face in a black-and-white movie on television when the Saturday Mets game was rained out, but in person it was stupendous.

Reagan shook my hand and asked how I was doing.

"I'm fine, fine," I said, with a smile on my face so big I could've swallowed my ears.

Margiotta then asked him how he was holding up with all that was going on outside.

"Well," he began in that wonderful baritone of his, "if you're in this game, you've got to let it roll off you like water off a duck."

Although I'd heard the expression before, coming from Reagan the words sounded like they should be etched in granite somewhere. One thing was for sure: I would never forget them.

Years later, in the Oval Office, I told the story to another president.

★ / ★ / ★

JOE MARGIOTTA RAN the Nassau County Republican Party from 1967 to 1983. He stopped running it only because they arrested him. He went to jail for mail fraud and an insurance kickback scheme. Somehow the arrest and conviction didn't alter the way many Nassau Republicans thought of him. For them, he was just as beloved behind bars, though presumably less able to get your nephew a job in the waterworks.

★ ∫ ★ ∫ ★

I WAS A pretty good student in high school, and this was in spite of the fact that I don't remember a single book being in the house the whole time I was growing up. This isn't a knock on my parents at all. First of all, neither of them had a lot of leisure time—Dad working two jobs, and Mom with her hands filled with us—but reading was also not a priority. Mom read her *Reader's Digest*. Dad got his news from the papers like everyone else, but the bulk of his intellectual stimulation came from people. He talked with his peers, his workers, the guy at Brothers All Market on Main Street, Hugo's Barbershop in Soundview, or the lady down the block he passed on his way home. That's how he learned about what was happening in the town, across the country, and throughout the world.

Much like the forty-fifth president of the United States, my father had what I'd call a living library. He kept names and faces in his head the way I keep books on my shelf. He could meet someone he hadn't seen in thirty years and know everything about them—their name, their wife's name, the color of that dog they used to have. I've tried to do the same thing over the years, but I'll never be as good as he was.

The irony of it was, however, though little emphasis was placed on reading in my house, getting an education was of paramount importance. My parents knew that college was the ticket out of the working class, not from personal experience but from empirical evidence in the lives of others in our station. They watched as the children of our neighbors succeeded, and they wanted that for us.

Looking back, my parents' insistence on education, and how that journey unfolded for me, is a remarkable phenomenon that was not at all uncommon. Because of our parents' hard work, a countless number of young Americans were blasted into lives of expensive suits and summer homes and cars that cost three times what my father paid for his house. That rocket ride took us into the stratosphere, a height from which our roots became small and insignificant.

I might not have even been on that rocket, however, if it weren't for Cynthia Magazine and her Entenmann's cheese Danish.

Todd Magazine, and I'm not making that name up, was my friend in school. When I went over to Todd's house, he'd always be at the kitchen table studying, and there'd always be an Entenmann's box on the table.

"Sit," Mrs. Magazine would say. "Have a piece of cake."

It was the type of psychology that Jewish mothers have implemented over the centuries. It worked like a charm.

And so my reading life began. Because of where I'm from, and Long Island's role in what some say is the greatest American novel, F. Scott Fitzgerald was one of my early favorite authors. Along with *Gatsby*, I devoured *Tender Is the Night* and *This Side of Paradise*. Fitzgerald, however, was only the appetizer. The main course was served in the Port Washington Public Library. I'm going to beat my chest a bit here but only because I give the credit back to where it's due.

I've probably read two thousand books cover to cover in my lifetime; I average about sixty a year. You never know when something good will become an obsession. I have been a very big believer in audiobooks since the late 1970s. I'd buy books on audiocassette from Barnes and Noble and from a company called Recorded Books. I would listen to audiobooks in the car or in the gym. When they invented the iPad, I'd read the book on the device while listening

38

to Audible (owned by Amazon) at one-and-a-half speed. I listen to about three hours of audio on a two-hour flight. I dedicate one and a half to two hours every day to reading. It's what I like doing. That's my jam, bro. And it's all thanks to Mrs. Magazine and her Entenmann's Danish.

★ ❘ ★ ❘ ★

DONALD TRUMP LEARNED a bit differently than I did. He had graduated from the Wharton School of Finance with good grades. The grades came in spite of the fact that he wasn't overly impressed with school. He had nothing against Wharton; he just thought what he read in the textbooks they gave him had little importance in his real life. Young Donald Trump had already worked hard for his father. He knew the rough-and-tumble world of real estate management and development. He'd worked with unsavory contractors and had tried to collect rent from deadbeat tenants. In one instance, he tried to show renters who were dumping garbage out of their windows how to use the incinerators in their building. Nothing he was taught at Wharton was going to prepare him for those experiences.

It was those real-life experiences, however, that motived Donald Trump to leave Queens and his father's business and strike out on his own. As I would, he wanted more than what his father had achieved. He could see the gleaming towers of Manhattan beckoning him.

In 1971, he moved into his first apartment in Manhattan, a studio on Seventy-Fifth Street and Third Avenue with a view of the water tank in the courtyard of the building next door. As he wrote in *The Art of the Deal*, however, he was more excited moving into that apartment than even into his triplex on top of Trump Tower.

New York City, even Manhattan, was then a rough place to live.

The city government was massively in debt, and its number had finally come up. Mayors had been rolling the unpaid debt onto the next administration for years, figuring it would just stay unpaid forever. A few years after Mr. Trump moved to Manhattan, the mayor of New York, the diminutive Abe Beame, had to announce before Congress that the city was in a fiscal crisis. The mood of the city was in free fall. Stories of murders, rapes, and layoffs—even of New York City police officers and sanitation workers—filled the newspapers. Workers in other agencies didn't fare much better.

As is often the case in these situations, the political class racked up a tab, and the working men and women of this country paid it.

It certainly didn't seem like a place to invest in.

"I worried about the future of New York City, too, but I can't say it kept me up nights," Mr. Trump writes in his landmark book. "I'm basically an optimist, and frankly, I saw the city's trouble as a great opportunity for me. Because I grew up in Queens, I believed, perhaps to an irrational degree, that Manhattan was always going to be the best place to live—the center of the world. Whatever trouble the city might be having in the short term, there was no doubt in my mind that things had to turn around ultimately. What other city was going to take our city's place?"

It was with that spirit of confidence that Donald Trump, then in his early twenties, just out of Wharton, began scouting out buildings for his first big foray into Manhattan real estate. He walked the streets of the borough, getting an up-close and personal view of the neighborhoods and buildings and, more importantly, the people who inhabited and worked in them.

He read a report in the *New York Times* about a block between Central Park West and Columbus Avenue at Eighty-Fourth Street. It was a tough area, dark and full of seedy hotels and seedier characters. Though in disrepair, the townhouses that lined the block were beautiful. With easy access to the park and, in some cases, with views of the Hudson River, their upside was huge. He also looked at riverside lots near the West Sixtieth Street train yards and at another rundown property on West Thirty-Fourth Street. When the city accepted his bid on the lots, Donald Trump had officially moved into Manhattan real estate, something his father, Fred, had never done. What Donald Trump was able to do by climbing out from under the shadow of his father—with almost no help, by the way, despite what you might hear in the press—is a little like burning down the house you live in and buying a bunch of lumber and nails to make yourself a new one. Had he failed, that would have been the end of it. Had he asked anyone's advice, they'd have called him crazy.

But he didn't. Though he wouldn't then develop the lots on Thirty-Fourth and Sixtieth, he came out of those deals and others wiser and with contacts that would help him secure another project. That deal would put him on the map and begin an incredible run that would eventually bring him the most exclusive piece of real estate in the world—1600 Pennsylvania Avenue.

The project that began the run was on another famous block—Forty-Second Street in Manhattan.

Though the Donald Trump of that early vintage behaved as if he were bulletproof, taking on Manhattan as though it were his birthright, much of that, I believe, was false bravado. People from Queens have always felt subordinate to the Manhattanite. It's something about living in the shadows of the city towers that fosters inferiority complexes. More than anything, young Donald Trump wanted to be equal to Manhattan's towers. He wanted Manhattan's respect. And yet, no matter how many buildings had his name emblazoned across them, no matter how tall and impressive those buildings were, no matter how big his lifestyle became, he never really felt he was given that recognition.

A need for respect in a man like Donald Trump can be a very powerful force. It can drive you all the way to the White House. When people ask me if Donald Trump wants to be loved or feared, I tell them neither. He wants to be respected.

★ / ★ / ★

B Y THE TIME I was in my senior year in high school, I was hoping to move out of the shadows, too, those of my blue-collar world. Not that I had a plan, mind you. I did, however, have some connections, or rather my father did from that living library of his. Good thing, too, or I would have ended up in Stony Brook University on Long Island, not that I have anything against Stony Brook. A lot of my friends went there.

Billy Tomasso, a friend of my father's, had gone to Tufts University, done pretty well in life, and remembered the school during fund-raising. Billy set up a meeting with the provost of Tufts. It was a pretty big favor. First of all, Tufts is rated in *Barron's* as a "most selective" school. Also, my grades weren't nearly as good as those of my brother, who got into Tufts three years before me strictly on academic merit. David graduated fourth in his class in high school. So I had to have some strings pulled, and then rely on my own sparkling personality. I took the Eastern Air Lines Shuttle up to Boston.

Sol Gittleman is something of a legend at Tufts. Along with being the provost, he taught some of the most entertaining courses in any college anywhere. Most of them filled up as soon as they posted, including one called America and the National Pastime.

I must have had the personality dial turned up all the way because Sol almost immediately took a shine to me.

"If we let you enroll," he said, smiling, "you'll have to take my course in Yiddish literature."

"Absolutely," I said, knowing absolutely nothing about Yiddish literature.

I would learn. Not only did I take "Yid Lit," as we affectionately called Sol's course, but I took two other courses taught by him. In Sol's introductory class, we used his textbook *From Shtetl to Suburbia* (*shtetl* is what they called the ghettos in Eastern Europe) and read books by Sholem Aleichem, Isaac Bashevis Singer, and Philip Roth, including *Goodbye Columbus*. In Sol's class on German writers, we studied works by Thomas Mann, Rainer Maria Rilke, and Herman Hesse, and read *All Quiet on the Western Front*, which President Trump once told me was his favorite book.

With Sol's help, I was no longer a schlemiel. I was on my way to becoming a mensch.

CHAPTER FOUR

THE GRAND OLD PARTY

"There's one born every minute."

—P. T. BARNUM

Rebel without a clue. Me in my Ghost Motorcycle sweatshirt on one of my Uncle Sal's bikes. (Scaramucci family collection)

The future president and his father, Fred, in front of Wolman Rink in Central Park, 1987. (New York Daily News Archive / Getty Images)

IN 1892, PHINEAS Taylor Barnum, better known as P. T. Barnum, purchased a large African elephant called Jumbo from the London Zoo. The name was a corruption of the Swahili word *jumbe*, meaning "chief." Barnum shipped Jumbo to New York, where he instantly became a sensation. The *New York Times* dedicated half of its front page to the elephant's arrival. Barnum's circus, with Jumbo as the main attraction, sold out venues like Madison Square Garden. The elephant became the most famous circus attraction in the world. For Barnum, Jumbo was worth his weight in gold.

Sadly, Jumbo's time in the spotlight was short lived. In 1895, only three years after the elephant came to America, he was dead. While Jumbo was being loaded onto a circus train, a freight train struck and killed him. According to Barnum, his prized attraction died saving the life of a young calf elephant. Though Barnum's version of Jumbo's demise has been challenged over the years, the lie did nothing to diminish the elephant's legend. The word "jumbo" became a proprietary eponym that described anything large in size (which would not include me). Even after his death, the elephant continued to draw fans.

In 1894, flush with cash he made off of the elephant's celebrity, Barnum donated a huge sum to a university of which he was a trustee. The money went to build a museum for his artifacts, one of them being Jumbo, whom he had stuffed and mounted. Here our story takes another unfortunate turn. In 1975, a fire burned the Barnum museum to the ground, destroying all of its contents including Jumbo's remains. Still, the name lived on. The university adopted it, which gave birth to one of the more paradoxical college team nicknames: the Tufts Jumbos.

When I arrived, however, the irony that a liberal bastion like Tufts had an elephant as its mascot was lost on me.

Located right outside of Boston, just 2.2 miles from Harvard Yard, Tufts has one of those beautiful red-brick New England campuses with walkways and leafy trees that turn burgundy and gold in the fall. For an Italian kid from Port Washington whose father worked on Bar Beach Road and thought the university's name was spelled t–o–u–g–h–s, the campus might as well have been, even with my brother landing there first, on the surface of the moon.

Many of my classmates were members of the liberal East Coast elite. They'd gone to the best prep schools in the country, eaten at the best restaurants, and shaken hands with senators and movie stars by the time they were just teenagers. Others were less ostentatious but still came from means and had a liberal bent that was nurtured at the school. In looking back, old Jumbo and I might have been the only Republicans on campus, and, actually, I didn't know yet if I was one or not.

Politics aside, it was finances that separated me from my classmates.

For many of my fellow students, the $14,000 tuition bill, a fortune back then, was something that Daddy and Mommy took care of. They didn't need to take out big loans the way my brother and I did, and they didn't think much about their own finances.

David and I, on the other hand, always had to think a few steps ahead. We had to worry where the money was going to come from. So we worked.

★ ✦ ★ ✦ ★

I TELL PEOPLE that I got "academic religion" when I was at Tufts. Actually, the moment of divine intervention happened in the house on Webster Avenue. I'd always been a pretty good student in public school. I'm blessed with a good memory, and I would do just enough work to cruise through my classes. I was home from college my first semester when the tuition bill came to the house. I watched as my dad cashed in a life insurance policy to pay it.

"I can get you through the first couple of semesters," he said. "But of course you'll have to borrow."

That had a great impact on me. It was in that moment I went from being a knucklehead Guido, tooling around in my Camaro doing push-ups in the disco parking lot, to becoming a dedicated student. If my dad was going to sacrifice his life insurance, the least I could do was give him a return on his investment.

It wasn't a huge sacrifice on my part. I liked college, and guess what? When you pay attention in class you have a better-than-even shot at learning something.

There were several economics professors who had a great impact on me. Dan Ounjian was my faculty advisor, and Linda Datcher Loury taught the history of labor economics. One of the first African American women on the faculty at Tufts, Dr. Datcher Loury was sharp tongued and funny, and she had an encyclopedic knowledge of social economics. From her, I learned of the history of union formation in the 1920s and '30s, the sharing and returns on capital between labor and management and/or capitalists. I have congenitally always been prounion because my father was in one. Without question, unions created an economic environment that was beneficial to the growing middle class. I'm the product of a well-organized union and a very good public school system. I learned about the struggles my father and the guys he worked with had gone through to be paid a fair wage in the '60s. I am a Libertarian more than anything else, and I believe in good policy to help motivate the working class.

Both Datcher Loury and Ounjian were liberal. The only professor I had who was conservative was an Austrian gentleman named Henry Delfiner. Dr. Delfiner's class laid out the template for the great economic thinkers, men like Ludwig von Mises, Fredrich von Hayek, and J. S. Mill. Delfiner understood how fascism could rise, having experienced it as a young Austrian in the 1930s. He understood the basic axioms of human nature.

Through my experience at Tufts, I came to realize that capitalism, much like the United States of America, was founded on a struggle between two opposing viewpoints, and that struggle— whether it was between Federalists and anti-Federalists or workers and their corporate bosses—made each side stronger.

I learned that confrontation and adversity keep systems alive. It's the struggle that keeps them adapting.

In my opinion, government spends too much of its time trying to fortify equal outcome. In reality, there are no equal outcomes. Even in a communist system, there's a thin layer of people at the top who are taking all the money from everybody else. Castro, one of the last great communists, lived in a mansion on the water in Cuba. What government should be trying to do is create some evenness of the playing field. So irrespective of your family economic status, you have a shot at rising in class, at rising in opportunity.

As my conservative voice began to take shape, especially when it came to economics, I was also having my conservative viewpoints challenged and interrogated at Tufts. Some professors railed against the corporate tax cuts Reagan had made in 1981, and they beat up on Wall Street every chance they could. Outside the classrooms, in the bars and residence halls, I was hearing similar pronouncements.

Other students told me Ronald Reagan, who'd been a kind of hero to me and my parents in Port Washington, was a lunatic. They said he was a brash, intellectually incapable movie star who didn't belong in politics. They told me people had only voted for him because of his media appeal and that they were worried he was going to get us killed because he might say the wrong thing to the Iranians or prematurely launch a nuclear weapon. Sounds a lot like what they said about President Trump.

For the most part, the students and faculty at Tufts had come to enjoy the leafy liberalism of suburban Boston, where the world's problems were far away and money would solve the ones that snuck through the gates. I probably would, too, if I'd been raised there.

I wasn't. I carried a sense of pride in the United States of America because of the people in my family who came before me. My grandparents had suffered hardship to come to the country, and then worked unbelievably tough jobs so they could stay. They faced discrimination, the storefront signs that read "No Italians Need Apply." They raised my parents with the hope that they'd be able to attain more than they had, and eventually my father did. My father went to work every day proud to be doing what he was doing, secure in the knowledge that a better life was waiting for him and his children because of it. A lot of my friends at school had never experienced that. My Uncle Sal knew this all along.

"There is no better education than the one you got at Ghost," he once told me.

★ / ★ / ★

At one time, and for a couple of decades, anyone who owned a Harley motorcycle within a five-hundred-mile radius of Ghost Motorcycle in Port Washington knew about Uncle Sal and his shop. Sal DeFeo is a legend. He's ninety-one and he still rides, though he needs a sidecar now for stability. When he ran his shop (it closed in 2000), he was both revered and loathed, depending on your tolerance for the sound that comes out of motorcycle pipes. The shop derived its name from Sal's Harley, which was white. The local cops took to calling him "ghost" on the radio as the white blur would fly past them, never to be caught.

I worked at Ghost on and off from when I was thirteen to when I went off to school in Boston. My parents weren't thrilled that I spent so much time at Uncle Sal's shop; they thought it was a bad influence on me. Maybe it was. At Ghost, however, I dealt with customers who crossed all lines of race and class, everyone from Hell's Angels to rich dentists, to some of the prettiest girls on Long Island, to Billy Joel, who was there all the time. I learned about business, and how to sell. I learned about what was fair and what wasn't. I also learned how to shoot craps, which we did after work every Thursday night.

Working at Ghost taught me about life in a way that no schooling ever could.

When I was seventeen and got my driver's license, I started doing deliveries for Ghost. Uncle Sal called the first one I did "a rite of passage." The address where I was to drop off the bike was 131st Street and Park Avenue in Harlem.

The year was 1981, and Harlem on 131st and Park wasn't exactly the leafy campus of Tufts. According to police statistics, 1980 had been, up until then, the worst year for crime and murder in New York City's history, numbers that would only increase throughout the decade thanks to the crack cocaine that decimated the inner city. I knew that 131st and Park was about as inner city as neighborhoods came.

"Don't worry," my uncle said. "You're not going alone."

I had no idea how to get to 131st and Park, and there was no Waze or GPS back then, of course, but Uncle Sal was my Google

Maps: "Go through the Midtown Tunnel straight to Park Avenue, turn right, and start counting," he said.

I arrived at the location a little early—the guy whose motorcycle was in the back of the van was supposed to meet me on the corner. While I was waiting for him, a shifty character walked up to the van. He knocked on the window.

"What do you have in there?" he said in a threatening way, peering into the back of the van.

I reached around to the back of my seat and grabbed Chico's collar and pulled him up so his nose was pressed against the window. Chico was the shop's Doberman pinscher, and a lovely dog if he knew you.

"This is what I got in the van," I said, with Chico adding an exclamation point to my sentence with a perfectly placed growl.

★ / ★ / ★

B Y THE END of my junior year at Tufts, I started to become aware of how the other half lived. In 1985, I studied at the London School of Economics for the months over the summer and saw much of Europe, including the USSR. When I worked at the White House, CNN would publish and retract a story that said I colluded with a Russian investment fund. I'll tell you more about that later, but the only connection I had with Russia came during my junior year abroad.

Though I got to travel some of the world, the road map that led me from polyester to wool suits appeared in an article in *Time* magazine. The piece was about Wall Street law firms in a bidding war for new lawyers. Cravath, Swaine and Moore, maybe the most prestigious law firm then in the country, had just increased the starting salary of a first-year associate to $65,000 a year. In 1986, to a twenty-two-year-old kid, sixty-five grand sounded like today's NBA signing bonus. My father was only making $40,000, tops. I'd gone home between my sophomore and junior years and worked with my dad. Even though Gotham Sand and Stone paid sixteen dollars an hour for the work—a generous wage in 1984—I wouldn't do it again if you threatened to run me over with a cement truck. When I came out of that experience I had even more appreciation for all the hard work my father had done to raise his family. I also knew I was never going to go to work wearing work boots again. I knew in my heart that I was meant to be a suit-and-tie guy. Shined loafers. Nice watch. I had undergone an intellectual awakening at Tufts, and now I wanted to put some of my newly acquired knowledge to work.

After the summer working at Gotham, I came back to Boston with the $65,000 figure dancing in my head and the idea of becoming a lawyer. It wasn't like I'd fallen in love with the law. I wasn't a Perry Mason fan, and Atticus Finch wasn't my hero. I just wanted to make more than my dad did.

WHILE I WAS plotting my climb into the moneyed class at Tufts, Donald Trump was quickly ascending to the top of New York real estate development. He was also making a name for himself as a champion of the regular people.

In the 1970s, when I was still in junior high, there was an ice skating rink in Central Park called the Wollman Rink. It was about the size of a baseball diamond, built right on the southern tip of the park. I could get there in an hour on the LIRR. From center ice, you could see skyscrapers through the leafless trees and get a rare view of the stars if the skies were clear enough. Couples and families would skate over the ice. It was a nice place to go after you'd seen the Rockefeller Center tree and the Christmas windows on Fifth Avenue.

Then, in 1980, the city shut the rink down for repairs. The tubes that ran underneath the ice to keep it cold weren't working anymore. So rather than opening the world's shallowest swimming pool, Mayor Ed Koch had the thing roped off and closed to the public. He said the repairs would take two years and about $4.7 million. They had to lay some good old Port Washington concrete over the ground, then freeze a little water on top. Easy, right? If the city kept its promises, he said, the public would be skating again by 1982. I was just getting to high school then, around the age where I could start going to the rink on my own, that is, if I had liked to ice skate.

Two years went by, and the rink never opened. Mayor Koch announced that they'd need another few years on the project, even though he was already severely over his budget and hadn't made any progress. This time, he said, they'd use a new chemical called Freon, which he thought would save resources and be a little less cumbersome to handle when winter came around. I'm not sure what kind of open government bidding system led him to that decision, but just about everyone knew it was a bad one. Unfortunately, they couldn't do anything about it. City governments don't feel the pressures of the free market, so they're more apt to go for silly, expensive things like a Freon system.

It's not like people will move away over it.

By 1985, the project was about $12 million over budget and the rink showed no signs of opening. The city around the rink wasn't in any better shape, and the city government was only a decade removed from the crippling debt crisis that had struck in the '70s. Storefronts were empty. Drug deals were rampant. No one had much faith that the mayor would be able to get a window fixed at City Hall, much less lay new pipes under an ice-skating rink. The government was struggling, and the working-class citizens of Manhattan, Long Island, and Brooklyn were paying the price.

Donald Trump knew that, and he saw an advantage. He had taken advantage of the city's downturn already, having bought up several properties around Manhattan and turned them into some of the nicest buildings on the island. As the city's overall fortunes began increasing, so too did Donald Trump's.

Oddly enough, in 1980, when Mayor Koch announced that the city was shutting down the Wollman Rink and rebuilding it in two years, Donald Trump had just broken ground on Trump Tower. Both projects were set to take about thirty months to complete. But only Trump Tower was finished on schedule. It came in on budget and on time in 1983.

Over the years that followed, Trump watched from his apartment window while the Wollman project sank further and further into disrepair.

Just as he'd done with New York City real estate, he waited for his moment. There would come a time, he knew, when the city was at its weakest and he could step in. Optics would be important.

Soon he found his opening. The city announced one morning in the spring of 1986 that it would scrap the work it had done so far on the rink and start over from scratch. That'd be a few million dollars down the drain and some contracts voided, but they didn't care. As I alluded to before, when you're in government, you don't have to care about our money.

Still, when it comes to public works, the government is usually the only game in town. They've got a monopoly on building and spending, and there's nothing we as citizens can do about it other than vote. And even that only happens once every few years. Donald Trump felt this frustration mounting, and one day in May he wrote the mayor a letter.

"Dear Ed," he wrote. "For many years I have watched with amazement as New York City repeatedly failed on its promises to complete and open the Wollman Skating Rink. Building the rink, which essentially involves the pouring of a concrete slab over coolant piping, should take no more than four months' time." Yikes, right? I remember reading that in Boston and chuckling. Even the *Globe*, which typically sticks to its corner of the country, covered it. Trump went on to talk about the city's responsibility to its citizens and how it had failed them. "I fear that in two years there will be no skating at the Wollman Rink, with the general public being the losers," he wrote.

Then came the offer.

"I am offering to construct and pay for a brand-new Wollman Ice-Skating Rink and have it open to the public by November of this winter. I would lease the rink from the city at a fair market rental, and run it properly after its completion."

Trump sent that letter on May 28, 1986. He didn't release it to the press or tell anyone about his offer. He knew he'd come off petty and arrogant if he tried. Somewhere in his mind, though, he must have known that Ed Koch would. When the mayor's response came by return mail, it showed up in the papers the next day. Koch said he wouldn't let Trump run the rink, but he offered to accept a $3 million donation and let him supervise the construction. The guy even quoted a Bible verse about blind charity. Had he been up against anyone else, maybe that would have worked. But people were too fed up with the city's incompetence. They wanted an outsider to root for, and they'd found one in a brash developer from Queens.

Even the press loved it.

When *Newsday*, my hometown paper, found out about the offer, they were ecstatic. "Let's have him go at it," they wrote in the back pages. "After all, the city has proved nothing except that it can't get the job done." The *Daily News* went after Koch for his "phony objections," and the *Post* called the Wollman project a "13-year multimillion-dollar debacle."

As Donald Trump said later when he recounted the incident in *The Art of the Deal*, it was the press that finally applied enough pressure. To quote him, "The only thing guaranteed to force [politicians] into action is the press—or, more specifically, fear of the press. You can apply all kinds of pressure, make all sorts of pleas and threats, contribute large sums of money to their campaigns, and generally it gets you nothing. But raise the possibility of bad press, even in an obscure publication, and most politicians will jump."

Ed Koch finally approved the offer, and begrudgingly agreed to let Donald Trump take the helm of the Wollman Rink project. By June, Trump had negotiated a deal in which he would put up all the money for the job himself, then have the city reimburse him the $3 million he'd spent once the project had been completed. There's a story about the details of the deal in his book, which I remember reading with astonishment.

Apparently, Trump had originally offered a deal in which the city would owe him nothing on completion of the project, and he'd make back what he'd spent with profits from the rink. The city wouldn't allow it, and instead offered him a $3 million reimbursement check for nothing.

This, as he points out in his book, is a deal you'd never make in a business environment. When you don't know the quality of the product that someone's going to deliver, you're meant to put as many conditions on them making a profit as possible. That's as true with stocks as it is with contracting. But the city didn't do that. They had no incentive for profit, so they offered Donald Trump a deal that was quite bad for them. This was a holdover, I think, from the competitive bidding process that governments typically use to determine who gets which contracts. This process ends up being a system of handshakes and backroom conversations, all funded by taxpayer money. Politicians and the contractors who work for them don't care much about profit, because their products don't have to compete in the market. So they've gotten perfectly used to offering lump sums regardless of how well the process ends up going. Had Donald Trump filled the Wollman Rink with Jell-O and left for Argentina—which, he says in the book, he'd have done if the rink didn't come out as planned—the city still would have owed him the $3 million! They offered a bad deal, and Donald Trump took it. As he'd say often on the campaign trail a few decades later, "No one knows the system better than I do. And that is why I alone can fix it."

Over the next few months, he supervised the job personally. Often, he'd visit the workers at the construction site and make sure everything was moving along, just the way he'd seen his father do in Queens. He talked to the guys who were laying the pipes and pouring the concrete, making sure there was adequate leadership down on the floor. He also decided to forego the city's Freon system and use brine instead—just salt water that's cold enough to make ice. What's important, I think, is that every step in the process brought a press conference. The press, as he noted at the time, couldn't get enough of the story. Papers from as far away as Miami—and Boston, where I was following it with excitement—dedicated whole spreads to the saga.

Here, I think, is where Donald Trump displayed his genius for branding and marketing for the first time. He could have completed the project quietly, ignoring hundreds of calls from the press in the process, but he didn't. Instead, he decided to let the public watch. He used his platform to set the incompetence of government and the ingenuity of free enterprise against each other, and the results were exactly what he wanted. He sent a message that people didn't have to go to the government for help—that they could rely on people who were more like them and, by extension, themselves to get things done.

Donald Trump knew how to fix the system, sure, but he also knew how to make people realize just how wildly screwed up that system had become. He understood, even back in the '80s, that people need a good story to make sense of the world. And that's exactly what he gave them. Good versus evil, proficiency versus incompetence, greed and power versus values and a good work ethic. By the time the project was complete—four months after he'd made the deal, and about $750,000 under budget—he'd become a hometown hero. The Wollman deal led him to appearances on morning shows, nightly news broadcasts, and eventually interviews with shock-jock disc jockeys like Howard Stern. Doing the interviews, he learned what appeals to people. They like funny stuff, and they like being told a few good stories. No one should be surprised that he treated the 2016 campaign like a few hours of smashmouth talk radio.

If you take a few courses in American history, as I did when I was at Tufts, you find that ascending to the presidency involves as much reliance on chance as it does skill. No one can predict how public opinion will have shifted by the time the race comes along, or what people will be tired of or hungry for.

Running for president is like riding a wave. You've got to find the right one, then hang on for long enough to reach the shore. Most candidates—the Mitt Romneys and Hillary Clintons of the world—find a good wave early on. They decide they're going to run when they're about four years old, then structure their lives around it. The problem comes when they have to pivot. As soon as they see a slight change in the wind, they try to jump on a different wave because they think it's bigger or better. As anyone who's ever been surfing knows, that kind of lack of commitment will lead you straight to a wipeout.

A candidate like Donald Trump, who's only going to come around once, picked his wave in the '80s and stuck to it. The public was getting tired of politicians talking to them in euphemisms, and dissatisfaction with Congress and Washington was just beginning to build. So he started taking small shots at the politicians. The Wollman Rink was one. Then he rode that wave up through the rise of shock-jock radio and reality television, and emerged fully formed onto the presidential debate stage. The other candidates never had a chance. The best candidates want to be themselves, not what they think the electorate wants them to be. Frankly, Reagan, Obama, and Trump all have that in common.

I'd been on a pretty good wave myself. It wasn't going to deliver me to the White House, but it got me a good score on my LSAT and accepted to six out of the seven law schools I applied to. The one I would pick would change my life in a way I could have never imagined. And it was only right down the road from Tufts.

CHAPTER FIVE

GOING TO HARTFORD

"He was wearing my Harvard tie. Can you believe it?
My Harvard tie. Like, oh sure,
he went to Harvard."

—LOUIS WINTHORPE III,
Trading Places

I was the first member of my family to graduate from an Ivy League school: Harvard Law! (Scaramucci family collection)

On top of the world! Donald J. Trump relaxing in his living room, January 1992. (New York Daily News Archive / Getty Images)

THE QUOTE "History doesn't repeat itself, but it does rhyme" is often attributed to Mark Twain. As with much of what's attributed to him, however, there's no hard evidence Samuel Clemens ever said those words. Twain is one of those figures who seems to get smarter the longer he stays dead. Just like Yogi Berra, new phrases of his appear from beyond the grave. Whoever said it, however, there's a lot of truth to it, especially when it comes to Ronald Reagan and Donald Trump. The two presidents are not clones, but if you listen, you'll hear a similar tune being played by the two.

For example: back in the '80s, terrorists groups were beginning to emerge, using violence to achieve their political ends, and no one thought Reagan was the right man to deal with them.

Sound familiar?

By April of 1986, tensions between the United States and Libya had become unmanageable. The countries were at each other's throats. The head of Libya, a dictator named Muammar al-Qaddafi, and his regime had been sponsoring terrorist groups in Britain and the United States since the '70s, making them responsible for uncountable deaths. The Irish Republican Army, the Black Panthers, and several Muslim terrorist cells in the Philippines had gotten money from the Qaddafi regime. They'd used that money to build bombs and buy weapons for their strikes.

In 1985, a terrorist group sponsored by Libya had bombed two airports at the same time. One was in Rome, the other in Vienna. Five American citizens died, and the United States tightened sanctions against Libya in response. It's not unlike the way we handle Russia or Iran today. They orchestrate or allow attacks on us, and we make it hard for them to participate in the international economy. This is exactly what the Marshall Plan was put in place to do—provide economical means for countries to use when resolving disputes so they don't have to do it with world wars.

But in this case, it didn't work. In March of 1986, Libyan ships clashed with the American Navy off the coast of Tripoli, resulting in the loss of four Libyan naval vessels. A few weeks later, terrorists bombed a dance hall in Germany where US soldiers were known to hang out. For Reagan, this was one strike too many.

He responded by ordering air strikes against Tripoli and Benghazi, two strongholds of state-sponsored terrorism. As the bombs fell on April 14, he addressed the nation on television, saying, "When our citizens are abused or attacked anywhere in the world, we will respond in self-defense. Today we have done what we had to do. If necessary, we shall do it again."

I watched that address from a dorm room in Boston. I remember feeling a sense of pride, not only that a man I'd once stood just a few feet away from was at the helm of the United States but that he was asserting our might to the world with a calm, measured grace. This was the opposite of what the pundits and columnists had expected from him. In fact, if you'd listened to them, you'd have thought Reagan was going to ride into Libya with a bomb between his legs and a six-shooter in either hand, yelling and screaming the whole way down. It's sad that it often takes a conflict—an actual invasion, replete with blown-up buildings and loss of life—to prove the pundits wrong.

But that's what happened to President Trump on April 13, 2017, nearly twenty-nine years to the day after Reagan's strike on Libya, when he dropped the deadliest nonnuclear bomb in our arsenal on a series of tunnels in Afghanistan. The Pentagon had received intelligence that members of ISIS had dug the tunnels around the country and used them to move around freely and execute strikes. They were choking the region like a pathogen, and they needed to be eliminated. So President Trump made the call and addressed the nation. Within hours the tunnels had been eliminated, and ISIS had been severely weakened in the area. It was the beginning of a nearly full retreat by the terrorist group. It's funny how you don't read more about that in the press.

Combined with the retaliatory air strikes against Syria a few days earlier, the dropping of the bomb was an enormous win for what you might call the Trump Doctrine. Unlike its cousin, the Bush Doctrine, this hasn't been proclaimed formally or written down anywhere. But it does comprise a few main tenets, the first and most important being that the United States will no longer be pushed around on the world stage. For too long, the United States has allowed terrorism to fester and rogue governments to finance international gangsters. We've made so many empty threats that our new ones don't mean anything anymore.

Beyond his talk and intimidation tactics—which, I'll argue, are more calculated and important than you realize—Donald Trump is a man who understands action. That comes from cutting deals in New York. I would know. If I sit down across the table from a guy who's walked away from a negotiation he wasn't happy with before, I know he's not bluffing when he threatens to do it this time. If I try to screw him over on the price of a company and he calls me out for it and shames me among the business community, I'll know I can't try that again. Trump said to me more than once, "If you're not ready to walk, you are not ready to negotiate and you will end up begging." That's him to a "T." Remember, this is the guy who in his first few months eliminated ISIS.

Donald Trump brought a man of action's sensibility to the presidency, just the way Ronald Reagan did in 1986. He took advantage of his standing in the world as a loose, take-no-prisoners negotiator, and he proved that the rumors were true. That's important. And it worked. There hasn't been a chemical weapons attack in Syria since those bombs fell, and ISIS is in ruins, little more than a few scattered cells looking for a leader. We shouldn't be complacent, of course, but we should call a victory a victory.

I'm not saying President Trump is the second coming of Ronald Reagan because he's far from that. What I'm saying is that we can learn from the overzealous and unhinged reaction to Reagan. We can see and read about how people discounted him as an outsider and a Hollywood lunatic, then try not to do it again. As Mark Twain (probably) said, there are no exact repetitions in history. But there are rhymes. And to my ears, the circumstances surrounding Trump and Reagan rhyme about as well as the words "Ronald" and "Donald."

I WAS ACCEPTED to Harvard Law on Ronald Reagan's seventy-fifth birthday, February 6, 1986. When I told my mother, she was so proud of me she immediately picked up the phone and dialed a friend.

"Anthony's going to Hartford," she said.

N OT TOO LONG ago I did *Real Time with Bill Maher*. It took stones. Not exactly like speaking at the Conservative Political Action Conference. In spite of the fact that he is left of Karl Marx (but also Libertarian on a few issues), Maher was pretty gracious to me, although he did zing me a couple of times. I mentioned that I was in Acting Attorney General Rod Rosenstein's section at Harvard Law and he thought I was name-dropping—not Rosenstein's, the university's. He rode me pretty good about it. I didn't mind; it was funny.

With me on the show was former DNC chairperson Donna Brazile, whom I've known and liked for a number of years, and David Frum, a writer for the *Atlantic* and an avowed Trump hater. The discussion started good-naturedly, with ribbing back and forth. Then Frum asked me a question that came out of left field. Obviously, he had planned the ambush and was waiting for the moment to spring it on me. The question was about the sale of my company, SkyBridge, to a Chinese company. Frum inferred...no, actually, he said that I leveraged my access to the president to inflate the price of my company. His question was not only factually inaccurate; it was mean-spirited and cowardly when you consider the setting in which it was asked. Much to Maher's dismay, I got into an argument with Frum. I was pissed. Among other things, I told him he was sanctimonious and culturally elite. Unable to come up with anything original, he stole Maher's line and said I was name-dropping Harvard.

Frum went to Harvard Law also. Unlike me, however, he doesn't have to tell people he did. You see, he comes from a wealthy Canadian family, and in the circles he travels telling people you attended Harvard is like showing them the label on your Savile Row suit jacket: it just isn't done. Besides, at the country club, dropping the "H bomb" doesn't quite have the same cachet as it does at my uncle's motorcycle shop.

After Maher's show, I found myself self-editing Harvard out of my interviews. In one, I even lamented the fact that I felt like I wasn't allowed to tell people I went to Harvard Law anymore.

When I came to writing this chapter, I thought: Screw that. I'm proud to have attended Harvard, and I'll tell anyone I want. I was the first in a family of generations of people who worked with their hands to go to an Ivy League school. Where I come from, going to Harvard was a big deal. Even going to Hartford was.

★ / ★ / ★

S O WHERE WAS I? Ah yes. I remember the moment when I walked out of my old world, the one I grew up in, and had my first glimpse of the gilded tower of my new one. It was that summer between Tufts and Harvard. I'd typed up my résumé on my Panasonic electric typewriter, went to the library to make copies, and dropped by Harvard Law School to pick up an alumni directory. I then searched for all the contacts who worked in finance and headed out to pound the pavement for a summer job. I was on my way to take the city by storm.

I hopped on the train in Port Washington to Penn Station in New York and took the subway down to Wall Street. I didn't even consider that some financial firms might be located elsewhere in the city. As it turned out, I didn't have to search very far to find what I wanted.

I started at the very bottom of Wall Street and planned to work my way up. One Wall Street is an art deco building right out of Ayn Rand. At the time, it was called the Irving Trust Building and was home to a number of prestigious law firms, including the white-shoe firm of Hughes Hubbard and Reed. In the late 1800s, Charles Evans Hughes, one of the founding partners, was the chief justice of the Supreme Court, not that that meant anything to me then. Filled with both a twenty-year-old's confidence and stupidity, I took the elevator up, marched right up to the receptionist, and asked to see the man with the name I'd circled in the alumni directory.

"Do you have an appointment?" the woman at the desk asked.

And then it happened. Dressed in a blue polyester suit, a tie my mother picked up for me at the mall, and shoes that I'd shined that morning, I was about to step through the looking glass.

"No," I said, "but I've just been accepted to Harvard Law."

The two words, "Harvard Law," were like a golden key to a private club that up until then I'd only seen in movies or read about in books.

The receptionist rose from the desk and disappeared behind oaken doors. In just moments a man in his forties with a golfer's tan and a pinstriped blue suit was shaking my hand. He led me back through the plush carpeted hallways to a corner office.

"How can I help you?" he said with a voice as smooth as the fourth green at Winged Foot.

"I need a summer job," I told him.

"I can hire you as a paralegal. Eight dollars an hour," he said.

Though I was wearing a polyester suit, and standing in a corner office for the first time in my life, I was still the kid who built the biggest paper route in Port Washington.

"Can you make it ten?" I asked.

THE INTERNSHIP AT Hughes Hubbard and Reed turned out to be a mind-numbing, soul-crushing, and career-questioning experience. HH&R had the contract for Frank Lorenzo's Continental Airlines–People Express merger-and-acquisition deal, which was a big thing at the time. My job was to read and organize contracts, sale-leasebacks, and airline-equipment lease and loan agreements. This was the age before PCs. We worked on a word processor and faxed everything. I put in sixteen-hour days for sixty days straight. No days off. For all of June, July, and half of August. While my friends were out on the beach in Hampton Bays (the blue-collar Hampton), or while my cousins were playing practical jokes at Ghost (one of which was hooking up a car battery to the door handle of the bathroom!), I was sitting in a back office in front of a stack of papers that never seemed to get any smaller. It was like being a sixth-century monk. If that wasn't bad enough, I was working alongside a fourth-year associate from the firm who was doing the same thing that I was. At some point, the thought came to me that working at Gotham would have been better. Well, almost. But the experience at HH&R got me thinking about whether or not I wanted to spend three years in law school to end up like the fourth-year schlub who was working next to me.

Still, by the time September came and school started, I was sitting in my first class, pencils sharpened. My newfound resolve lasted about two months. The first months of law school are like learning a new language and mastering a centuries-old philosophy. Though my classes were interesting, I quickly realized I was about to put a whole lot of work into something that I didn't have my heart in. Besides, I'd taken out a big loan. Why waste money on something I knew I didn't want to do? During my first break, I headed home to tell my parents. Rationalization swirled around my head. I wouldn't have been the only one to quit, I'd tell them. Clarence Darrow quit law school! So did FDR and Vince Lombardi. Vince Lombardi! The man who said "once you learned to quit it becomes a habit" quit! Vince Lombardi may have had an Italian mother, but he didn't have my Italian mother. There were two things that my mom was very good at: ironing and guilt. So when the school break ended, I was on my way back to Harvard.

My first year in law school I lived in Hastings Hall. Built in the 1880s in a medieval design, and located right on Massachusetts Avenue and next to Hemenway Gym, the hall was a coveted location. If you won the housing lottery, you ended up in Hastings. If you lost, you ended up in the Gropius Complex, a group of interconnected residence halls with monastery-sized rooms. A national tragedy. Living at Hastings, on the other hand, was like having a suite in an elegant, old hotel. My roommate and I each had a bedroom, and we shared a living room with a working fireplace, and a communal kitchen downstairs. If the accommodations weren't opulent enough, my roommate, a very nice young man from Hong Kong, dropped out after the first semester and I had the place to myself.

But it wasn't just the luxuries of the crib that drew me in. The first year of law school has a workload designed to wear you down. My darling New York Mets went to the World Series and I only watched maybe an inning or two on a thirteen-inch, rabbit-eared television. This is where my blue-collar work ethic paid off. Much of learning the law is based on trial and error. You find out what is salient, and what not to waste your time on. I was good at that. That talent was simply common sense, born out of a sandpit in Port Washington and passed down. As my time at Harvard went on, I took classes such as Trial Advocacy with the venerable Charles Nesson, Constitutional Law with Laurence Tribe, and Ethics and Tactics in Criminal Law with Alan Dershowitz, with whom I'm still friends. I studied under Philip Heymann, who taught classes in criminal law and became deputy attorney general for Bill Clinton's administration. Despite the heady trappings and famous legal minds, I brought to each of my studies a working-class toughness and sensibility that were a match for even the most sophisticated setting or scholastic pedigree. I also brought along a sense of humor.

★ / ★ / ★

IN MY LAST year of law school, I took a tax law class taught by a visiting professor from Boston College Law School. By then, I had solidified my reputation as a serious class clown. I had already gotten a job offer from Goldman Sachs (more on that to come), and I was spending less and less time at Austin Hall, where the classes were held, and more time at Hemenway Gym.

Part of the requirement for the tax class was a mandatory oral session where you'd stand and answer a series of the professor's questions on cases and other topics he would pose. His first mistake was telling us that we would be called in alphabetical order. I figured out how many classes it would take for him to get to the Ss and promptly skipped every one of them. By the time it was my turn, I'd almost completely forgotten about the professor, his class, and certainly my oral session. A friend of mine gave me a heads-up that very morning. I woke up late, didn't even shower, and walked into class wearing my black motorcycle jacket, a Rangers T-shirt, and a Mets hat. At that moment, it occurred to me that, despite what Woody Allen might say, just showing up wasn't going to mean anything. I didn't study at all and knew nothing about the cases he would undoubtedly ask me about. I needed a strategy, and I needed one quickly. Perhaps drawing from my Trial Advocacy class, I decided to deflect and distract.

As it happened, the professor had gotten his hair cut over the weekend. We used to call the style he was sporting a Tupperware haircut because it looked like someone had put a bowl over his head and just trimmed what was sticking out. I was sitting next to my friend Kevin, who was a very, very smart guy. He had just returned from Oxford, where he'd gone on a Rhodes Scholarship.

"What would you give me if I just started talking about his haircut when he calls on me?" I whispered.

"Five bucks," Kevin said.

I took my Mets hat off, handed it to him, and told him to tell the person in the row next to him. When the hat came back to me, it contained $140 in crumpled fives and tens.

By the time the professor called on me, the whole class was in on the joke. As big as my reputation as a cutup was, I don't think any of my classmates believed I would do it. When the professor called my name, the class was still in anticipation.

"Professor," I said. "Before I begin my dissertation, let me first say that's one of the finest haircuts I've ever seen."

The room exploded in laughter, and the professor went beet red. For a second, I thought he was going to kick me out of the class.

No such luck.

I don't know if you remember the movie *Paper Chase*, where John Houseman plays the Harvard Law professor, but Houseman could have gotten pointers from my tax professor. He roasted me like I was on a spit. And he kept going, and going, and going. At about the fifteen-minute mark of the lambasting, I knew I had to do something, or he might just run out the clock.

I looked down at the Mets hat in my hand and back up to him.

"Professor," I said meekly. "Allow me to apologize. I have 140 bucks in the hat; I'll give you half if you let me sit down."

Again, the class erupted in laughter. But this time, the professor laughed too.

"I tell you what," he said. "Give me all of it, and I promise I won't give you an F on the final."

★ ✦ ★ ✦ ★

I ALSO LEFT my mark on Harvard in a more substantial way. The *Harvard Law Record* is the oldest law-school newspaper in the United States. Student-edited and published, the *Law Record*'s masthead and bylines have included the names William Rehnquist, Ralph Nader, and Barack Obama. Though the editorial side of the paper was legendary, the business side wasn't so hot. They could write, but they didn't know how to sell advertising. I became the head of advertising in my senior year. Along with Jeff Moslow, a friend from school, I came up with an idea. Each year, large law firms would hold cocktail parties and interview sessions as part of their recruitment efforts. My idea was to cold call the firms and ask if they wanted to advertise the events in the *Harvard Law Record*. Every one of the firms wanted as many students as they could draw to the event, so it wasn't that hard a sell. Just about every one of the firms took an ad, and the *Law Record* was saved.

I N SEPTEMBER OF 1987, as I was starting my second year in law school, Donald Trump was first toying with the idea of running for president. He bought ads in three major newspapers around the country to "air his foreign policy views," said the *New York Times*. "There's nothing wrong with America's Foreign Defense Policy that a little backbone can't cure," Mr. Trump wrote. He added that America "should stop paying to defend countries that can afford to defend themselves." That was thirty years ago! The man hasn't wavered in his beliefs.

In New Hampshire, where the first presidential primary is held, a "Draft Trump" movement had begun. Mr. Trump's name recognition was already off the charts, and he had a strong showing in impromptu polling—he gave a speech in a restaurant in Portsmouth, New Hampshire, his first political appearance anywhere, and packed the house with followers and press. He even traveled to Moscow in the summer of 1986 to meet with the Soviet leader Mikhail S. Gorbachev to talk about the development of luxury hotels there. He also spoke with Gorbachev about nuclear disarmament. This was still during the height of the Cold War. Reagan had not yet called for Gorbachev to "tear down this wall." It's ironic that Trump's trip to the Soviet Union at a time he was considering a run for the presidency didn't cause a blink in the American press. How things have changed.

You'd have to imagine that the ads, the speech, and the trip to Moscow were all one big trial balloon. But knowing President Trump the way I do, I know the decision of whether he would run would come from his gut. In 1987, his gut wasn't convinced. "I'm not running for president," Mr. Trump told *Newsweek* in June of 1987, "but if I did... I'd win. There, I said it. I didn't think I would, but I did."

Mr. Trump went to the 1988 Republican Convention when George Herbert Walker Bush and Dan Quayle were nominated. He told me that when he looked around the Superdome in Louisiana, he said to himself, "I want this. This is something I want in my life." The great, interesting thing about Donald Trump is that he built his authenticity with his lack of programming, but at the same time always kept his eye on the target. He knew that someday he was going to run for president. This is very different from Mitt Romney, who was a guy—a very nice guy—but a guy who built a perfectly planned, hermetically controlled life to achieve that goal. In doing so, he missed the zeitgeist of our time, where Americans reject personality perfection and embrace flaws. They sense, these crazy Americans, when you judge them. Lesson to future pols: stop the judging and righteous superiority bullshit. The way politics seems to work is that there are these huge waves that come into the beach and politicians succeed or don't depending on their surfing skills. In 2016, Mr. Trump got up on his surfboard with his authentic character, his three wives, his children from three different marriages, his larger-than-life New York City lifestyle, and shot the barrel. What he did rises above politics. But he'd been above politics from the start. At that '88 convention he did an interview with Larry King.

"You know, wealthy people don't like me, because I'm competing against them all the time," Mr. Trump said to King. "When I'm in

New York, the people I really relate to are the taxi drivers, the vendors, people like that."

"Then why are you a Republican?" King asked.

"I have no idea," he said. "I believe in certain principles of the Republican party, but..."

THE '80S WERE pretty remarkable for Mr. Trump. He had purchased the iconic Plaza Hotel in Manhattan for $400 million and was in negotiations with Frank Lorenzo to buy the Eastern Air Lines Shuttle. He had already bought and lost a franchise in the now-defunct USFL. As the owner of the Jersey Generals, he paid huge salaries to top stars such as Doug Flutie and Herschel Walker. He was spending money like he was printing it, and there seemed no limit to his appetite for acquisitions. The bigger and more expensive the better seemed to be his motto. But even Donald Trump can be overleveraged. As the sun set on the '80s, Mr. Trump was about to stumble in the darkness.

In 1976, New Jersey voters approved a referendum to allow gambling in Atlantic City. At the time, Nevada had been the only state with legalized gambling. It was a very big deal. There were visions dancing in heads both in the gambling community and in Trenton, the state's capital, of untold riches. AC, as it was commonly called, was going to be as big as Vegas, only on the ocean and much closer to the big cities on the East Coast. For a while, it looked like those visions would come true.

The first casino in Atlantic City, Resorts International, opened in 1978. With a captive audience, it was a resounding success. Casinos bearing familiar names like the Sands, Harrah's, and the Golden Nugget quickly followed, and business in all of them was brisk.

One hundred twenty-five miles north, in his newly constructed masterpiece, Trump Tower, Mr. Trump was well along in his plans to get a piece of the AC action. He had been buying land in Atlantic City for years, and in 1982 applied for his first casino license. He entered into a deal with Holiday Inn, Harrah's parent company, to build a thirty-nine-story casino-hotel. Harrah's at Trump Plaza opened in 1984 as the largest casino then in AC. In 1985, he opened the Trump Castle Casino. A year later, he bought out Holiday Inn and renamed the casino Trump Plaza. For a while, Atlantic City and Donald Trump seemed like a match made in one-armed-bandit heaven. According to *Time* magazine, in 1989 gaming revenues in Atlantic City outdistanced the Las Vegas strip, and by a considerable amount ($2.7 to $1.9 billion). Mr. Trump not only stamped AC with his brand—which was now, thanks to Trump Tower and Trump's casinos, known around the world—but he brought Vegas-like sizzle to the seaside town. In 1988, he promoted the Mike Tyson–Michael Spinks title fight at Convention Hall in AC, then the highest-grossing fight ever. He promoted WrestleMania IV and V. Muhammad Ali, Don Johnson, Barbara Streisand, and Jack Nicholson all came to watch the fights he promoted.

But the biggest act he booked was yet to come.

B Y THE TIME I graduated from law school, I had opened the door to a world of people who worked indoors, out of direct sunlight, and didn't lift anything heavy. I went to Harvard to put on an academic badge that indicated I was worthy of this world and talented enough to excel in it. It was a very wealthy world I had entered. For years to come, until May of 2016 in Albuquerque, I was steeped in the action of the economic elite, working with hedge fund managers, capital allocators, Masters of the Universe, as Tom Wolfe so aptly named them. I was in the salons of the wealthy. Five-star hotels. The best restaurants. Going to conferences, speaking at the World Economic Forum. I'd removed myself from the struggle of the neighborhood in which I grew up. I didn't do it because I didn't like my neighborhood; I did it out of my desire to be upwardly mobile, a desire to move between classes to reach a world I could have only imagined as a kid. Yet when I got there it was different from what I'd imagined. F. Scott Fitzgerald once said that the rich "are different from you and me." F. Scott was wrong about a couple of things, and this was one of them. They're not different; they're the same, only richer. Along the way, however, I also acquired the collective biases from the consensus of the wealthy who have, by and large for the last fifteen or sixteen years, misunderstood the struggle of the working class.

All of that was yet to come, however. Before I reached such rarified air, I almost choked on the fumes.

CHAPTER SIX

DOWN FOR THE COUNT

"Money never sleeps, pal."
—GORDON GEKKO,
Wall Street

"Many people are afraid to fail, so they don't try. They may dream, talk, and even plan, but they don't take that critical step of putting their money and their effort on the line. To succeed in business, you must take risks. Even if you fail, that's how you learn. There has never been, and will never be, an Olympic skater who didn't fall on the ice."

DONALD J. TRUMP

IN JULY OF 1989, I took the bar exam, and in August I started working at Goldman Sachs, valuing properties and stocks in their real estate division. I had to go through a series of thirty interviews the previous November and December before Ken Brody, the head of Goldman's real estate division, offered me the position. The job meant looking at lots of spreadsheets, macro software equations on Lotus 1-2-3 and Excel, stuff that I wasn't all that fond of. It was boring. I'm good at numbers, not great. I'm much better with people. Still, I was working for Goldman, where I wanted to be, and, I guess, I kept hoping things at work would get better. Though I had no intention of practicing law, I'd taken the bar for the same reason I'd gone to law school—because I didn't want to disappoint my mother.

Now, I know I've already told you about my mother, but she was such a motivating force in my life I'm going to give you a fuller description. My mom's the type of mother who would iron your pants while you had them on. She ironed my underwear when I first went away to college. She uses guilt the way Bruce Lee used nunchucks. What's the old Jewish joke? My mother doesn't do guilt trips; she owns the travel agency? That's my mom. Remember Danny Aiello's sick mother in Sicily in the movie *Moonstruck*, the one who's dying and guilting him to come home? That's my mom. When I told her I was thinking about dropping out of Harvard—just thinking about it!—you would've thought I said I was joining ISIS. She threatened to kill herself right at the table.

She had the same reaction when I told her I was thinking about not taking the bar exam. I didn't have a choice, really.

"Mom, all right, all right! I'll take the test!"

Anyhow, being a lawyer would sound cool at cocktail parties. *He's managing a few billion in assets,* they'd say. *But did you know he's also a lawyer?*

But even my mother's nuclear-capacity guilt couldn't coax me out of the water. I prepared for the test by spending the beginning of that summer on skis behind my father's fishing boat in the Long Island Sound, or giving my uncle a hand at the motorcycle shop, or with my friends out in Hampton Bays at the Boardy Barn or the OBI (the Oak Beach Inn) or some other beach hangout. Many of my friends had stayed in town for the seven years I'd been away. Some had built successful businesses for themselves hanging drywall and paving driveways. Others commuted into the city and worked in offices. Most of them would go on to marry local girls, and live on budgets, in homes with mortgages, and for the most part, they were happy. Most of them still live there. Even though I've traveled the world and worked in the White House (they call me a big shot, to break my balls), so do I.

I guess I was a little overconfident when it came to the bar exam. I was working more on my tan than on memorizing civil procedure, contracts, or constitutional law. Still, if you had asked me right up until the moment when I walked into the exam room, I would have told you I was going to water ski my way right through the test. When I sat down, however, I had a twinge of doubt. Maybe even a touch of guilt for not doing the work.

Afterward, I thought it was going to be close. I'd gotten stuck on a couple of multiple-choice questions, and guessed on an essay question.

A few weeks later, I found out I was right. It was close. I needed 660 to pass, and I received 656, also known as one freakin' question short. I was angry, but only for a second, and only at myself. I knew the failure was all on me. I could have prevented it if I had studied a little harder and water skied a little less.

Within hours, I'd signed up to take it again the next February.

THE NEXT DAY I passed a newsstand on the street. There was a front-page headline on the morning edition of the *New York Post*.

"The Hunk Flunks," it read.

I was mortified. Not only had some reporter at the *Post* managed to find out about my failure; they'd run it on the front page. Even worse, they were making me out to be some mindless dilettante who was only known for his charm and good looks.

Okay, I knew the headline was about John F. Kennedy Jr. John-John was about my age and height (give or take seven inches), and we'd taken the bar on the same day. He was working for the Manhattan district attorney at the time and needed to pass the exam to keep his job. When he didn't, it became a national news story. This, in a sense, was comforting to me. I might have blown the exam, I figured, but at least I could go to work every morning at Goldman Sachs where they didn't care if I got my law license or not.

I kept my appointment to take the exam again. Aside from keeping my dear mother breathing, I did it because I wanted to close out the lawyer chapter of my life. I'd read enough Greek tragedies in college to know that pride and hubris get you nowhere in life. (Usually, they get you wandering around the city with your eyes clawed out.) I could act like I was too good to be a lawyer all I wanted, tell as many old lawyer jokes with the guys from my department as I could think of—Why did the lawyer who fell into a shark tank come out without a scratch? Professional courtesy—but I would still be a failure if I didn't try again.

So I studied a little harder this time and took a few extra practice exams. I blocked out some time every night to go over statutes and old cases. Somewhere down in Tribeca, John F. Kennedy Jr. was doing the same thing. He and I hit the books while working full time—he at the DA's office, I on the seventeenth floor of the Goldman building on Broad Street. I would imagine John Jr. felt just as determined as I did when we both strode into the exam room again in February. I cracked open the exam booklet and began writing. Before I knew it, six hours had passed by the time I'd finished the last essay. The next day, I took the multistate portion of the exam as is customary and thought I did fine.

I didn't run into JFK Jr., but I would imagine he felt a little better too. There's a confidence that comes over you on the second try. You start to feel like the universe owes you a win.

A few weeks passed. I kept up a steady pace at Goldman, often working ten- and twelve-hour days. Snow began falling, and the weather got worse, almost mean. I was living in a small apartment then on Eighty-Fourth Street, not far from Donald Trump's first apartment. One night, coming in from the cold of the street after a long day, I found my exam results in the mailbox. I tore open the envelope, looked at my score, and felt my stomach sink.

I'd scored lower than the first one. I'd failed again.

In the office the next morning, I told the guys the news. They clapped me on the back and told me it was all right. Sometime that week I found out that Junior Kennedy had failed again too. I don't know why, but it was a small consolation to be failing in relative privacy, and then watching him do it in front of the nation. Although they wouldn't say it out loud, I could tell my parents were disappointed. Mom didn't even try to guilt me. My friends told me I was better off without it. I was a Wall Street guy now, they said. I should forget about the whole lawyer thing and stick to what I was good at.

So I did. Through the winter and spring of 1990, I went into the office every day and worked harder than I ever had before. Even though I found the job difficult, I was where I wanted to be—even Hollywood knew that Wall Street was the place to be. A few years before, when I was still in law school, Oliver Stone screened his new film at the Harvard Square Theater. I identified more with Bud Fox than Gordon Gekko, at least back then, but I was intoxicated by Stone's depiction of Wall Street. I was also working for a bank just about everyone who went into finance wanted to work for. What motivated me the most, however, was watching as my brother's Wall Street career took off.

As I mentioned, David had graduated number four in his class in high school and graduated from Tufts with an engineering degree. Then he worked a couple of years at Grumman, the aircraft company. Just as I had felt interning for the law firm, he hated his job. So he went to NYU, where he got his master's in finance. With that master's in hand, and on top of his engineering degree, David's résumé went to the top of the pile of every finance firm at which he interviewed. He took a job with Drexel Burnham Lambert, where he worked as a mortgage-backed bond trader. By the time I graduated from law school, David was crushing it, on his way to making seven figures and managing a $2 billion bond portfolio. Even though I was in the real estate division, and felt out of place there, and wasn't making anything near what my brother was making, I saw myself on the same path as the one my brother was on.

★ ✦ ★ ✦ ★

E VEN THEN, WHEN I was busier than I'd ever been, I kept up my childhood habit of reading a few papers cover to cover. Since leaving Long Island, I'd graduated from *Newsday* and the *New York Daily News* to the *New York Times* and the *Wall Street Journal*. The latter is practically required reading when you're working at Goldman. Free copies floated around the office like bath toys in a kid's tub; you couldn't escape it. Every day, it seemed, I read about the conflicts that were brewing overseas and about threats to stocks and holdings in the newspapers.

Over the next few weeks, the papers starting reporting on the conflict in Kuwait. The first Gulf War was beginning, and the specter of the United States getting involved in the war had a devastating effect on financial markets.

My division at Goldman responded to the downturn with layoffs. Mike Fascitelli, the man who hired me, was put in charge of deciding whom to fire and whom to keep. At the time, I was working under two vice presidents, one of whom thought I was an idiot. No matter how hard I worked for her, her opinion of me changed not one bit. That was strike one. Strike two was the economic downturn the country was then experiencing. Sometimes in business you have to make hard calls, and Mike was there to make them. With two strikes on me, I walked around him on eggshells for a whole year. Then on February 1, 1991, Mike invited me to his apartment on Jane Street. I knew this couldn't be a good thing. I went down after work, around seven o'clock, as he had asked. As I walked from the subway, I felt the weight of my failing the bar twice and a hundred thousand bucks in student debt behind me. I was dragging it all like a sled. We sat in his living room, which had a window that looked out on the piers in the Hudson River. He got to the news quickly, which I appreciated.

"Anthony," he said. "You're a good guy, everyone likes you, and you're a hard worker. But even with a ton of training, you're only going to get slightly better. What I have to tell you is painful for me…"

★ ❙ ★ ❙ ★

ALL OF FEBRUARY and into March I looked for a job. Long before I ever owned a cell phone, I carried a pocket filled with quarters to make network calls to friends and people I met in school and in my short Goldman career, anyone who might offer me a lead. I interviewed at First Boston and several other banks and came up empty. With the economy languishing, it wasn't the best time to be looking for a job. I had to move out of the apartment on East Eighty-Fourth. Paying $1,400 a month in rent was out of the question. I took a place in the basement of a private house in Tarrytown, New York, for $600 and rode the Metro North train to the city each morning.

By the beginning of March, I began wondering if things were ever going to get any better.

One day, while I was on the train, I read a story about Donald Trump in the *Times*. Though Mr. Trump had been a mainstay in the tabloids for most of the '80s, the broadsheets had mostly steered clear of him. Yes, there was the occasional mention or profile, but the *Times*, particularly, owned a disdain for news generated by Donald Trump. But now, Mr. Trump, his high-profile divorce from Ivana, and his financial troubles in AC, made him front-page news. Up until he was president, and even after he took office, Mr. Trump read the *New York Times* cover to cover every day. He called it his "hometown paper." But back then, like now, it seemed that his hometown paper was joyfully predicting his demise. The story I read that day was about his father, Fred, buying $3 million in casino chips at the Taj Mahal so his son could make an interest payment.

When the Trump Taj Mahal casino and resort opened in 1990 it was the largest casino in the world. It was also the most expensive, costing a staggering $1 billion to build. Just for Mr. Trump to pay the interest rates on the loans he had taken out, gamblers would have to lose $1.3 million a day. For a guy who doesn't gamble, Donald Trump had made a bet of monumental proportions on the Taj Mahal. It didn't take long for the business to begin to collapse under its own weight. As it did, the knives of the Trump haters came out quickly. Forgotten were the fifteen thousand jobs he created for the city, the hundreds of millions in tax dollars and other revenue that went to the state, and the untold amounts of money his gamblers spent in other establishments in AC. All you heard was that Donald Trump was greedy, his ego had caught up to him, and his business sense, if he ever had any, had escaped him. The truth, however, had more to do with outside influences than anything in Donald Trump's personality. In 1987, the stock market crashed. The country had entered a recession. Gambling revenues that skyrocketed through the late '80s had flattened out in the '90s. Atlantic City and the state of New Jersey had overlooked a critical aspect of running a successful gambling town—business diversification. Vegas was suffering through the same recession, but it had begun developing nongambling attractions. People who couldn't afford to gamble their money still came to Vegas to see Cirque du Soleil and Penn and Teller, or to eat in restaurants featuring celebrity chefs. To top it off, Mr. Trump opened the casino right in the middle of the Iraq War. People were watching Scud missiles on TV instead of taking tour buses to play the slots.

Stories in newspapers told of him being billions in debt. The countdown for the collapse of his casino ventures, an event that would likely be the end of him financially, was chronicled in the *New York Times* for everyone to see. I'd read *The Art of the Deal* in the summer of '88 when I was a summer associate at a law firm called Kaye, Scholer, Fierman, Hays and Handler, located on Park Avenue just a few blocks from Trump Tower. Sometimes on my way to Penn Station and the train home, I would walk by Trump Tower, and each time I did I was brought back to the first time I was in that building. It was Christmastime, not too long after it opened in 1983. I remember the towering glass of the façade that climbed to the sky, the atrium with the soaring ceiling, and the gold plating. I was awestruck. It was simply the most beautiful building I'd ever seen.

When I read his book I experienced a turning point. Although I might not have been able to build a tower, I wanted to dream big like he did.

But now here he was, on the front page of the *New York Times* and *Wall Street Journal*, worse off than me.

CHAPTER SEVEN

THE ART
OF THE COMEBACK

"My experience is that if you're fighting for something you believe in—even if it means alienating some people along the way—things usually work out for the best in the end."
—DONALD J. TRUMP,
The Art of the Deal

The Scaramucci's: brother David, sister Susan, Mom, Dad, and me. (Scaramucci family collection)

ALTHOUGH AMERICA DOESN'T own the patent on comeback stories, we've perfected the art. One of the biggest advantages our country has over others is that we accept people who are willing to take enormous amounts of risk. And when they fail, dust themselves off, and start over, we love them. Henry Ford, Sam Walton, Donald Trump, the names on the comeback list are countless. Our culture accepts risk takers and failure. Most of us have lived our own *Rocky* screenplay at one point or another and some more than once. We know what it's like to get up off the canvas.

In looking back, it seems almost ridiculous that I would have such a bleak outlook on my future. I was a healthy twenty-seven-year-old with a couple of impressive degrees in my back pocket. But a negative voice started to play on a loop in my thoughts. You're not good enough, it said. You'll never be good enough. You can't even keep a job.

With that voice playing incessantly, one morning that July I read that John F. Kennedy Jr. had managed to pass the bar. I closed the paper and got back to work. Hearing about him passing made me feel even more like a failure.

Now, it wasn't like I was flat broke. Goldman had given me $11,000 in severance pay and three months of health care. I had a cushion to fall back on, and the thought even flashed through my mind to take a couple of weeks off, maybe head to Puerto Rico, and cool my jets for a while. Give me time to reassess.

I had loans to repay, however, and a neighborhood to answer to. I wasn't about to go back to my uncle's shop, face my friends and cousins, and admit that I'd failed.

I might have been wearing a suit and tie, but at heart I was still a Guido. I was still the kid in the Camaro wearing chains and an open shirt that had the Playboy bunny insignia on the chest—you know, where the Polo guy goes? You can say what you want about me being a Guido (and people still do), but inside every one of us is a fighter. I don't know for sure, but I think at some point I reached in and pulled out my inner Guido. Right about then, I started to hear the *Rocky* theme in my ears. It was faint at first, but with each day I pounded the pavement, each quarter I dropped into a pay phone, each interview I showed up for, the music got louder.

Two months after Mike Fascitelli fired me, I dropped a quarter in a phone, one of scores of times I did, and dialed a friend's number.

"Know of anything?" I asked.

"Matter of fact," the friend said, "They're hiring at Goldman."

I thought he was joking, breaking my shoes, and I wasn't laughing. "Come on."

"They are," he said. "Institutional sales."

My next call was to Mike Fascitelli. Before Goldman, Mike worked at McKinsey and Company, a huge consulting company that does research and analysis into business practices and corporate culture, among other things. A lot of psychological stuff. After he'd fired me, he'd given me this whole schtick about the stages I was going to go through.

"Stages?" I'd asked.

"Yes, SARAH."

"Who's she?" I asked.

"The five stages of adapting to change," he told me. "Shock, Anger, Resistance, Acceptance, Hope."

"Uh-huh."

"Right now, you're probably shocked, maybe a little angry."

Well, he had me there. I was angry, but I knew enough to keep my mouth shut. It helped that I liked Mike, and knew he liked me. As far as the rest of SARAH, I don't remember resisting for long, or even accepting my fate. Instead, I only remember being embarrassed.

When Mike answered the phone, I asked him if he would give me a recommendation for the job opening at Goldman.

"You're a good guy, and a hard worker, Mooch," he said. "You were just mismatched with me. I'd be happy to give you a recommendation."

The next thing I knew I was interviewing for the job, and on March 28 Goldman Sachs offered it to me.

Now, I'm sure that there are others who have been fired and rehired at Goldman. If there are, however, I doubt there are many. Guido or no, I knew one thing for sure: they weren't going to have to give me more than a second chance.

★ / ★ / ★

M Y FIRST DAY, I reported to Human Resources. Toni Infante was running HR for my division at the time. She told me she had good news. She was going to put me down as an interdepartmental transfer. This way, she said, I would never have to tell people I was fired.

"All you have to do is give back the $11,000 severance check," she said.

Toni's a wonderful friend, and we laugh about this now. But back then there was no way I was giving back the check. I needed it for living expenses and loan payments. And, drawing on my legal education, I knew there was also mental anguish involved.

"That's okay," I said. "I'd rather tell them I was fired."

My office was in the same building, 85 Broad Street, as my first go-round at Goldman. But instead of the seventeenth floor where I used to work, this time I would take the elevator all the way up to the twenty-ninth floor. And, as far as my career was concerned, the elevator continued to climb. From that moment, it was game on. I was all business. I'm a rabid New York Mets fan, but I couldn't tell you one player from the team from March of '91 through '95. All I did was work and breathe. I knew I had been given a second chance, and I wasn't about to screw it up.

I didn't. My new job fit my skill set. I had to develop relationships on behalf of the firm. Communication, marketing, and delivering information. I've always been able to talk to anyone and hold my own in the conversation. I could do more than just chitchat. I did my homework. I knew what I was talking about. It didn't take long before the feelings of being less than confident when I was out of work disappeared, and something close to the Mooch swagger appeared. Not that I was acting like a jerk. But I quieted that inner voice, and my natural mental state has always been a positive one. There was only one more thing that I had to take care of. In February 1992, I approached my new boss and asked him for two weeks off.

"To take the bar exam," I said.

Now, I had only been working for him for ten months. Two weeks off was a big ask. And he knew that I had already taken the test and failed, twice. I wasn't sure how he'd react.

"I'm glad you're doing it," he said. "You want to be known as a finisher, not a quitter."

I wanted to be a finisher. This time I hit the books hard. I took a bar examination tutorial course. I spent the whole two weeks getting ready, and, seeing how it was February, didn't once think about water skiing.

I never got to meet John F. Kennedy Jr. But if I had after I received my passing grade on the test, I would have walked up to him and slapped him a high five.

★ / ★ / ★

B Y 1991, THE press had Donald Trump's business career dead and buried. The obits ran in the papers just about every day. "The empire that Trump built is about to be dismantled," went the first line of an April 1991 *New York Times* story. The article went on to list the assets Mr. Trump would have to forfeit to the banks: His interest in New York's Grand Hyatt Hotel would go to Bankers Trust. Citicorp would take his stake in Alexander's, a department store chain in which Mr. Trump had invested. The Trump Shuttle airline would be portioned off with NWA Inc., parent of Northwest Airlines, and several dozen banks elbowing for their share.

The Trump Regency Hotel in Atlantic City was to be sold, with most of the proceeds going to Manufacturers Hanover.

And then there was his 282-foot yacht, which was about to go repo to the Boston Safe Deposit and Trust Company, a subsidiary of American Express. The yacht had marble-and-gold waterfalls, a formal dining room, gold-plated faucets, suede walls, and leather ceilings. He'd bought it for $30 million from the Saudi Adnan Khashoggi, who needed cash. I remember reading about the purchase in *The Art of the Deal*. I also remember reading about the boat in the *Doonesbury* comic strip. But now the yacht had set sail to Boston, with Mr. Trump left standing on the dock.

Many of the stories in the newspapers and magazines ran with photos of Mr. Trump. In each of them, he looks right at the camera and smiles. In *The Art of the Deal*, he wrote that he'd wondered what it would be like to lose everything, not because of the hardship he might experience himself, but to find out who was loyal and stuck by him, and who wasn't. Think of that. If he decided to dunk you, would you be able to stay loyal and close?

"Success," wrote Mr. Trump in his book *Surviving at the Top*, "so often is a matter of perception."

Almost immediately after the Taj Mahal opened, it became evident that the casino was not going to make enough to pay the bond payment. Shareholders hired Wilbur Ross, currently the secretary of commerce, who was an expert in distressed assets, to represent them in negotiations. He flew to Atlantic City in Mr. Trump's helicopter, which had "TRUMP" emblazoned on the sides. As the helicopter landed on a helipad near the boardwalk, a mass of press and onlookers descended on the helicopter, thinking Mr. Trump was in it.

"They were shoving video cameras at it... It was amazing the adulation he got from the crowd," Mr. Ross told the *Wall Street Journal*.

"It changed my whole opinion. That memory stuck with me and got me to the conclusion that the Taj Mahal stripped of Trump the individual would likely be a lot less successful than the Trump Taj Mahal with Donald."

Mr. Trump would prove Wilbur Ross right and all of his critics wrong. (The April 1991 *Times* story would be proved almost completely wrong. In fact, Mr. Trump sold his yacht to the Boston bank for a $15 million profit.)

By 1992, stories in newspapers and magazines about his comeback were even more prevalent than the ones predicting his demise.

"As nasty as the press can be," he told a *Vanity Fair* writer at the time, "they know that once they've cut you down the best story is to build you back up again. Piece by piece, deal by deal, a beautiful story is starting to emerge about me."

The Art of the Comeback

It was a story only Donald Trump could write. By 1989, he had reached the pinnacle. Everything he touched turned to gold. He owned casinos, a yacht, a fleet of flying machines, an iconic hotel, a tower known throughout the world, an airline, had two *New York Times* number-one best sellers, and condo buildings that people fought over to buy into. According to *Forbes*, he was worth around $1.7 billion—and that was in 1989 dollars. Two years later, after the bottom fell out of the real estate market, he was in a financial position from which no one is supposed to come back.

By 1992, however, he was on his way back and would be better than ever. Comebacks are for all of us, you and me.

In the coming years, the Taj would start making money and would eventually become the most profitable casino in AC, by far. The Taj, which everybody thought was a foolish, ego-driven white elephant, became Mr. Trump's cash cow, pumping millions into his private accounts. Atlantic City, too, staged a comeback. By 1996, the seaside gambling resort was raking in about $4 billion a year—30 percent more than the Vegas strip. Everything seemed to come back in an instant. Mr. Trump even bought back his 727 jet.

People who knew him knew that he wouldn't stay down for long; most were just amazed that he came back so quickly. Mr. Trump told a reporter back then that his mother and father were his biggest supporters and cheerleaders, even when he was at rock bottom.

"When the shit hits the fan," Mr. Trump remembers his father saying back then, "do yourself a favor. Go to a bookie and put a lot of money on Donald's head."

★ ✦ ★ ✦ ★

IN 1992, I made $260,000 at Goldman Sachs. I was twenty-seven. The following year, I was given a $100,000 bump in pay, and I didn't think it was good enough. Sounds like I was getting a little full of myself, right? When everyone you work with is making that much and more, however, it doesn't feel so outrageous.

Besides, I thought I had good reason to think I was being shortchanged.

By the last quarter of 1992, Dell Computer had reported fourteen consecutive quarters of rising profits. Partly the company's success was due to high-tech distribution and old-school customer service. But beginning in early 1993, Dell started to stumble. There were flaws in the laptop design and some risky investments that went south. The company desperately needed money.

In 1993, Michael Dell came to Goldman to raise capital. The Capital Markets division called our sales desk and asked us to sell a convertible bond they were putting together for him. A holder of a convertible bond can swap it for stock in the company anytime they want. It was the beginning of August by the time the bond was ready to sell, and most of my clients were wearing boating shoes and eating at the Palm out in East Hampton. I didn't care. I picked up the phone and started making calls. I knew this was a good deal for them because I had done my homework and knew Michael Dell was a masterful guy.

Dell had been a customer of Goldman since 1988 when his company went public. Throughout the late '80s and into the early '90s, he had gone from a startup out of his University of Texas dorm room (before he dropped out of school), to owning the fourth-largest computer company in the world. Dell's success was one of the reasons that IBM got out of the personal computer business. To get his company up and running, he once told me, he had to make 8,000 decisions, and 7,800 of them had to be correct.

I told my clients that Michael Dell was a steward of the computer business and that the bond was a "high coupon," a low premium with a good chance of converting into a lot of equity. In other words, a really good deal.

The investors agreed, and we were able to raise $250 million. With the infusion of cash, Michael Dell and his company shot up like a rocket and became one of the great stocks of the 1990s.

I'm not saying I did this deal all by myself. There were plenty of talented people who worked on it. My compensation, however, should have better reflected the success of the deal and my role in making it happen.

In hindsight, I might have been better off if I had just taken the hit and moved on. Sometimes it's better to lose the battle to win the war. I didn't just move on. Instead, I took my beef to my boss's boss. He looked at my numbers and agreed they weren't paying me enough. The word came down to my direct boss, who grudgingly increased the pay from $360,000 to $400,000. His attitude was that I should have been grateful for the job and that I had some pair of balls to be unhappy with the money he was paying me a little over one year into my Goldman career. Now, there's nothing wrong with fighting for what you deserve. But being cocky without experience is never a good combination. In twelve-step recovery, they use the word "TIME" as the acronym for Things I Must Earn. But back then, at twenty-nine, I wasn't going to wait around.

About that time, my father bought a new silver-gray 1992 Lincoln Continental with power steering. After decades working as a laborer and running heavy machinery and after his hearing started to fail because of the blasting, Gotham had given him a desk job. He was a natural manager and knew the product better than anyone. Then, when he was sixty-two, right around the time I got the job at Goldman the second time, they promoted him again, this time to the president of the company. After forty years of Chevys, and one brown Ford Crown Victoria, he bought the Lincoln because he thought that it was appropriate for his position. I used to make fun of the car—it was the size of a boat. To my dad, however, it was every bit as good as a platinum Rolls-Royce.

It was a good year for my dad. In 1992, he made the last payment on his thirty-year mortgage. We had a mortgage-burning ceremony.

I'd decided to go to law school because I wanted to make more money than my father. I shared this one-up complex with many in my generation. We wanted more, and we wanted it faster. And the lucky ones, like me, got what we wanted. But as I accumulated things—cars, houses, businesses—I was focused more on the hype and social status and began to forget the pride my father had behind the wheel of his Lincoln. Back then, I was solely thinking about more, and what was coming next. What came next was pretty remarkable.

CHAPTER EIGHT

BECAUSE
I'M AN IDIOT

Me with Mets manager Bobby Valentine. A small group of us bought the jersey that Mike Piazza wore when he hit the game-winning home run in the first Major League game played in New York City after the attack on the World Trade Center. It hangs in the Baseball Hall of Fame and is now on loan to the 9/11 Memorial & Museum. (Scaramucci family collection)

THERE ARE ACTUALLY two Wall Streets: the one that exists in the light of day, a caffeine-fueled, frenetic network of brokers, trades, deals, and a scoreboard that constantly shows the world whether you're up or down; and then there's the one that comes alive after the closing bell.

Back in the '80s, and even now to some extent, part of a broker's job was to entertain clients. David became very good at this aspect of his job. He was out three or four nights of the week, and then every night, with customers. Whether it was at Madison Square Garden to see the Rangers, dinner at Sparks Steakhouse, or late night at the topless dance club Scores, he was the tour guide and cruise director wrapped up in one. At least that's the way it started.

David and I are different in many ways. He was always a lot smarter than me, faster than me, and, adhering to the Leon Spinks law of big-brother superiority, he could beat the living daylights out of me.

One of the biggest differences was the way we partied. I am a certifiable lightweight when it comes to alcohol. My friends in high school took to calling me "Moses" because of my religious-like aversion to booze. One or two cans of Budweiser was my limit. David, on the other hand, was like a moth to a neon sign—literally. He started in high school with just beer. In college he graduated to some pot and a bit of cocaine. It didn't seem to affect him too much, at least as far as his studies went, but the seeds of alcoholism had started to grow roots. Once that happens, they tell me, it's only a matter of time before the booze and drugs have their way with you. David remained a weekend warrior in grad school, but when he took his first job on Wall Street in 1987, it was as though he sprinkled Miracle-Gro on his nascent addiction.

This was the era of Jay McInerney's *Bright Lights, Big City*, and it wasn't at all unusual for a vial of Bolivian marching powder to be in David's jacket pocket. I've never done illegal drugs in my life, not even pot. When I got in trouble working in the White House, stories ricocheted around the Twitterverse that I was high on coke. Not true. Fake news. I'll take a lie detector test if you don't believe me. But David tells me that coke and booze go together like peanut butter and jelly; that is, if the peanut butter allows you to drink about a gallon of Welch's grape jelly. Though coke made him feel invincible at first, soon he was doing it alone and paranoid in a dark hotel room. There is always a price to pay, and David had begun to pony up.

While David was in a hotel room snorting lines, his wife, Rebecca, and Victoria, their oldest daughter, were home worried sick. Rebecca lasted with David longer than she should have, but everybody has their limits. When she had had all she could take she packed her bags and left with Victoria. David came to my house in tears. "You have to stop, bro," I told him. "It's not just you that you're hurting."

His job, too, had had enough of the missing days and reports of blackout nights. Most of the time in these situations, at least in larger businesses such as Wall Street firms, the company is very supportive of an employee who wants help with a substance abuse problem. But it's not three strikes, you're out. It's one strike, you go to rehab, or you go away. David went to rehab.

I took the ride up with him to the twenty-eight-day facility in upstate New York. On the way, my brother was gaunt and worried. He was headed into the unknown and didn't know what to expect. We didn't realize that the driver of the car was listening to us.

"You're going to a place where you have to unpack your bags, and I don't mean your suitcase," he said. "You have some emotional baggage you have to get rid of." The driver, an older African American man, had been sober in AA for many years. In remembering that scene, David calls it "a God moment," meaning that it was too coincidental not to have been orchestrated by some higher power. I cried after I dropped him off.

When my brother came back, he was a changed guy. He stood up in front of his coworkers and asked for forgiveness. They welcomed him back with open arms. He began trading his position again and soon was promoted. He and Rebecca had two more children. He was a miracle, and I was never any prouder of him. What I've come to find out, however, is that alcoholism is a disease that never goes away. You can arrest it, one day at a time, but it's always there lurking, waiting for you to let your guard down. For seven years or so David was a model of recovery. Then his life might have gotten too good. He didn't think he needed to go to AA meetings anymore. Somewhere inside of him, his disease was rubbing its hands.

I tell this story with my brother's permission. I love him dearly and am very proud of him. He has used his experience to change and save lives. He has done God's work here on earth and is anchored by a real faith. He can also see right through any bull. In the summer of 2017, just before I was fired from the White House, we did a podcast together where he told his story of recovery. A couple of hundred thousand people and counting have listened to that podcast.

Trump, the Blue-Collar President

★ ∫ ★ ∫ ★

A BOUT THE TIME my brother went to rehab, I began contemplating a move from Goldman. Years later, President Trump asked me why I left a bank that had produced so many respected and uber-successful men and women.

"Because I'm an idiot," I told him.

The line wasn't original. Bob Rubin, Clinton's treasury secretary, said something similar first, I think. In my case, it was also not exactly correct.

In my five years at Goldman, I rose to the position of vice president of Wealth Management, where I was making $1 million my last year. In Wall Street parlance a million is called "a stick," and it's a benchmark. I'd wanted to work at Goldman for the cachet, the solidness of the company, and the money I could make, and I'd achieved all that I wanted. Along the way, however, I realized that I wanted more than what I thought the bank could offer.

I also knew that I was not going to rise very high at Goldman. Or, more specifically, I was never going to be a partner. There are a couple of different types of personalities at Goldman Sachs. There are the partners, who for the most part are wonderful, but, then again, they have everything to feel wonderful about. There are the journeymen, who are always jealous of the people who make partner; and then there were guys like me, who were outsiders. If you ask anyone who works for Goldman to verify what I'm about to tell you, you'll get denials up and down. Nobody there will ever admit to this, but if you're an Italian kid from working-class roots, there's a glass ceiling that you'll never be allowed to break through. That's the way it is. Maybe there's an exception or two, but they are merely tokens.

Even if they offered me the corner office, I wasn't going to be a token.

Besides, it had occurred to me that the happiest I'd been in my working life was the day I handed Mrs. Sheridan a copy of *Long Island Newsday*. I was an entrepreneur. I would never be truly happy working for someone else. Once I realized that, I was like a rocket on a launching pad during the countdown. There was nowhere to go but up, to places far from where I started.

I LEFT GOLDMAN ON November 29, 1996, and with my partner, Andrew K. Boszhardt Jr., opened a hedge fund called Oscar Capital on December 2. As soon as we opened the doors, calls started pouring in. Not about business, however. Goldman people would call and ask for us to send over a package of hot dogs. People called asking for Oscar Madison, Oscar de la Renta; somebody wanted to know how you get nominated. Even my kids were giving it to me. "Do you work with Oscar the Grouch?" they'd ask. We had had the best intentions in naming our business. We wanted it to contain letters from our last names, but BosScar sounded like some infection, so we dropped the B and S. We might have been better off dropping the whole idea. Then, after one week of doing business, things got even rockier.

On December 5, Fed chairman Alan Greenspan delivered a long, rambling speech that would have been quickly forgotten if not for two words it contained: "irrational exuberance." What he meant was that stocks had become too hot, and that the market, which had closed over 6,000 (6,000, how quaint, right?) for the first time that October, had gotten too big for its britches. Overnight, the Dow tanked. For a few days, it looked like Oscar really might end up in a trash can. But Greenspan was wrong, and the market quickly rebounded. For three solid years the Dow went straight skyward, and Oscar Capital grabbed hold of the rocket's tail.

Along with good fortune, we had a couple of other things going for us. My partner, Andy, was one of them. Eight years older than me, Andy is from a hardworking midwestern family and was imbued with the midwestern values of honesty and generosity. He had been at Goldman for about fifteen years and had worked for a man named Bob Steel in international sales as a wealth manager. Steel rose to senior partner at Goldman and together he and Andy made buckets of money. But then Andy started to get the itch. Like me, he knew he didn't have the personality to become a partner. He wanted to try something for himself. When he asked me if I wanted to come along, I jumped at the chance.

We'd also built some solid relationships with clients at Goldman, and they helped. One was with a man named Joseph E. Robert. Joe made a fortune in distressed commercial and residential real estate in the late '80s and early '90s and had sold his company to Goldman. Joe became a client of mine in the bank's high-net-worth practice. When we started our business, Joe gave us a $7 million seed. I used to joke with him that we put his check on the pizza oven, like the guys that open a pizza place do with the first dollar they make.

By New Year's Eve 1997, our fund was up 81 percent for our first full year in business. We had $200 million in new business in the fund. The year had gotten off to a rocky start. I remember reading the *Wall Street Journal* on the train into work each morning. Every day that first winter bad news stared back at me. But we had climbed the mountain, and the view from there seemed to stretch forever in every direction.

Although I have never fully completed the task, it was around this time that I began to grow up. When you're your own boss, you have to learn discipline and maturity, or you might as well pack it in.

But I didn't lose the Mooch. When you're a success you go to work because you want to be there, not because you have to, and that state of mind builds a tremendous amount of self-worth. It also feeds the ego—not a bad thing in proportion. Have you ever met a successful person who didn't have an ego? When you combine just enough ego with self-worth, and you add my personality, which some have categorized as "wacky," what's produced is a supercharged sales machine who might drive you nuts or charm you, or both. But I guarantee you one thing, you're not going to forget me. I was thirty-two, and I was just getting started.

★ ✒ ★ ✒ ★

O N THE MORNING of September 11, 2001, I was sitting in a thirty-fourth-floor conference room of Oscar Capital with my bag packed and a car waiting for me downstairs. I was booked on a ten o'clock shuttle to Boston. Back in those innocent days, you could walk right through the airport and onto the plane without so much as a second look from security. Just as I was about to leave my phone rang. "Turn on the TV," my mom said. "A plane flew into the World Trade Center."

Like just about everybody else, I at first thought it was a small plane that had hit the building. Then the second jet flew into the South Tower fifteen minutes later and I knew we were under attack.

Our offices were at 666 Fifth Avenue, ironically the building that was bought by Kushner Properties, Jared Kushner's company. We closed the office and everyone headed down to the street. There were no taxis or public transportation, so we began walking up Fifth Avenue toward Andy's apartment on Ninety-Second and Park. I remember at one point turning around and looking south and being able to see the smoke and flames from the fire at Ground Zero.

I stayed in his apartment the entire day, watching TV and waiting for them to open the bridges so I could drive home. Manhattan had been sealed tight. Manhasset, the town I lived in then (and now), is the rich cousin and neighbor of Port Washington. Manhasset has had a connection with Wall Street for a couple of generations—many of the people I knew and worked with lived there. Some of my best friends did.

It was evening when they opened the bridge. The images of the towering buildings collapsing played on a loop in my head. The terrorists had ripped a hole in the heart of our city and left a cloud of overwhelming grief and paralyzing fear. It seemed that everyone knew someone, or knew someone who knew someone, who worked in the towers. The attack had somehow managed to shrink New York City into a small town. I knew dozens of people from financial institutions with offices in the top floors of the building, firms such as Cantor Fitzgerald, Marsh and McLennan, and Sandler O'Neill. One of them was my friend Chris Quackenbush.

Chris was a founding principal partner of Sandler O'Neill and Partners, an investment bank and trading house. His office was on the 104th floor of the South Tower of the World Trade Center. Chris was a mentor to me and a dear friend for years. I'd like to think I'm a halfway decent guy when it comes to being generous. As part of Student Sponsor Partners, a Catholic organization that provides low-income students the opportunity for a quality education and one-on-one guidance, I'm a mentor to a kid name Errol from the South Bronx. I've helped him get through high school and college. But I was a cheapskate next to Chris. We'd joke about people who worked on Wall Street who wouldn't give a dime to charity if their lives depended on it. He called them "Marley," after the miser ghost from Dickens's *A Christmas Carol*. But Chris did more than just joke. He started the Jacob Marley Foundation, which, among other charitable acts, funded education for needy children. Chris would spend much of his free time with underprivileged kids, teaching them to read and taking them to Mets games. I have never met anyone more giving in my life. One of the best days we had together came the summer before 9/11. I'd introduced him to my friend Bobby Valentine, who was then the manager of the Mets. Bobby was hosting a charity golf event in Connecticut. Chris made a bid on one of the auction prizes, a trip to the All-Star Game as Bobby's guest. Because the Mets had won the pennant the year before, Bobby was the manager of the National League team. Chris won the auction, and he and his kids found themselves on the field in Seattle's Safeco Park, watching the Home Run Derby.

The new house that I had built was near the Manhasset train station. When I passed it that night the parking lot was filled with cars. It was late, well after the time that commuters would have stepped off the train and driven home to their families. Only later did I realize the significance of the full parking lot. Only later did I realize that one of the cars must have belonged to Chris.

Rumors circulated in the first few days after 9/11 that some who had gotten out of the towers alive had been ferried to hospitals in New Jersey. Out of the eighty-three Sandler O'Neill employees who showed up at the World Trade Center for work on September 11, 2001, sixty-six were still unaccounted for. Forensic teams had joined the search-and-rescue units at Ground Zero. A few of us jumped in a car and drove to Jersey. Maybe Chris had been knocked unconscious and couldn't contact his family. The rumors turned out to be false. None of the unaccounted-for survived. Chris's memorial was scheduled for September 22.

On September 21, the New York Mets hosted the Atlanta Braves at Shea Stadium in the first professional baseball game held in New York City after the attack on the World Trade Center.

At the time I had a suite at Shea. I called around to some of the families that I knew had lost loved ones and asked if their children would like to come to the game. These were people who were deeply grieving, many of them still in shock. Some were worried about a second attack, not an unfounded fear at the time. My wife and I argued over whether I should bring our son and daughter, AJ and Amelia, to the game. My kids would come, as did seven other children, along with some of the parents. One of the children was CJ Quackenbush, Chris's son.

The experience that night will never leave me. It was a game in a surreal atmosphere. Bagpipes played during the pregame, and people sobbed. The Mets came out wearing FDNY, NYPD, and Transit Police hats, and we cheered. Most of us were numb from the visual assault that came after the attack—the videos that play incessantly on TV, the walls filled with photos of missing loved ones. The family members still holding onto the impossible. The game itself was secondary to the overriding emotion.

That is, until about the seventh inning. At the stretch, the Mets were down 2–1. Liza Minnelli came out and sang "New York, New York." Liza Minnelli might not be the choice of a baseball crowd, but she knocked us out that night. The song became our anthem. Each time she sang the words "New York, New York," our pride swelled further. No matter where you were from, in Shea Stadium that night everyone was a New Yorker, even the Atlanta Braves.

In the bottom of the eighth, with the Mets still down by a run and a man on first, Mike Piazza stepped to the plate. The fact that Mike's Italian wasn't the only reason he was my favorite Met, but it didn't hurt. He's also a Hall of Famer and one of the best hitting catchers to ever play the game. The Braves pitcher was Steve Karsay, a New Yorker who grew up just a few miles from Shea in College Point, New York. But no one expected him to throw Piazza a meatball. Karsay was all business that night. With one out in the eighth, he had faced Edgardo Alfonzo, the Mets' second baseman. Karsay had Alfonzo down two strikes and then threw a pitch that a guy on the top row of the stadium could have told you was strike three. But the ump's right hand didn't move, and Karsay nearly jumped out of his spikes. Rattled, he then proceeded to walk the second baseman. With Piazza, however, he seemed to have settled down. The first pitch he threw him was a blistering fastball on the inside corner. Strike one.

I remember looking at the kids in the suite, some of whom wore Mets hats, eating hot dogs. A normal sight at any other time, but not now. Their eyes held a dullness, as if they had pulled down a shield, God's way of protecting them from the thought of a lifetime of loss. How could a kid ever imagine a parent under the twisted girders, the broken blocks, the smoke that rose from the pit and pile, the images seared into their consciousness? How, I thought, would they ever be whole again?

Piazza hit Karsay's next pitch into the light stanchions past the centerfield fence. For us there who watched that night, the ball traveled even farther than that. It soared out over Queens, streaked over the East River, skied above downtown Manhattan, and landed right in the middle of that smoky pit. It landed with a message to those who attacked us: we will be back, it said, and better. If you ask me, America is like a big Italian family. We have our disagreements. Some of us get so mad we don't talk to each other for years. But try to hurt us, and see what happens.

In the suite, we jumped, hugged, and screamed. For a precious few moments all that mattered on the earth was baseball, and that our team was going to win. And for a precious few moments, seven children were relieved of unimaginable grief.

A few years ago, a small of group of us, including Tony Lauto, an investment banker friend; Jim McCann, a founder of 1-800 Flowers; and a friend who wants to remain anonymous, bought the jersey that Piazza wore that game. The Mets had sold it to a collector for reasons I still don't understand. We donated the jersey to the 9/11 museum at the World Trade Center site in downtown Manhattan. Every July, around induction ceremony time, it hangs in the Baseball Hall of Fame, where it deserves to be.

In spite of the way it seemed then, the world continued to turn, and the years went by. CJ went to the University of North Carolina, his father's alma mater. He wanted to work in Major League Baseball and got a job with the Phillies when he graduated. He didn't stay in Philadelphia for long, however. His heart was somewhere else. Today he works for the New York Mets, in the client services area. And though the team now plays in a new stadium, there are times Citi Field can still feel to him like a September night at Shea.

A NDY AND I sold Oscar Capital to the money management giant Neuberger Berman in November 2001. We'd settled on the price with Bob Matza, who was the president and chief operating officer of Neuberger, before the terrorist attack. The stock market stayed closed for four days after the attack, and when it opened it promptly dropped 600 points, which back then was an enormous decline. Still, Bob stayed true to the deal, and we finalized the sale in those financially uncertain weeks after 9/11.

I stayed on at Neuberger as a managing director. I was happy at the firm, but having been my own boss, I didn't know how long I would have stayed happy. As it happened, I would never have to find out. In 2003, Lehman Brothers bought Neuberger. In the space of two years, I'd gone from owning my own hedge fund to working for a bank with a legendary past and a future so bleak its demise would literally shake the world.

But before Lehman crashed and sank on the rocky shore of the financial crisis, I would chart my own path.

CHAPTER NINE

THE APPRENTICE

"Anyone who thinks my story is anywhere near over is sadly mistaken."

Donald J. Trump

I N MAY OF 2002, Donald Trump stood in Central Park looking at his Wollman Rink. He had taken control of the property in 1987 as part of his deal with the city in the form of a long-term lease and had been overseeing upkeep and maintenance of the rink ever since. Thanks to the brine system he'd installed under the ice, the upkeep typically didn't involve much other than routine repairs and pipe replacements. The rink had become a steady source of income for him, much to the chagrin of Mayors Ed Koch and David Dinkins, another tough-on-business Democrat, who took over from Koch in '89. Compared to the rest of his empire, the cash flow from the skate rentals and concession stands was minuscule, but the property was a winner. And Mr. Trump loved winners. Plus, he'd learned from the crash of the early '90s that it helps to have assets and revenue streams spread across the board. Never again would he put all his eggs in one basket.

But in May, there was no ice-skating or people buying hot dogs at the concessions. Instead, there was dirt. Lots of dirt. There were also fake palm trees, vines, coconuts, and a big wooden stage where center ice would have been. A banner reading "SURVIVOR" was hung from it. Donald Trump had been asked a few weeks earlier by Les Moonves, the head of CBS Entertainment, for permission to use the Wollman Rink to film the live season finale of *Survivor,* and, sensing that it might be good for both the rink and his brand, he said yes. Trump arrived that day in May to find the place transformed into a jungle, with cameras and sound equipment all over the place. There were even bleachers for the live "studio" audience. Standing in the center of it all was Mark Burnett, a tall, skinny Englishman whom Trump had heard of but had never met.

Mark Burnett was a man with whom you could be easily impressed. By the time he found himself in Central Park with Trump, he had already been a paratrooper in the British Army, a scuba diver, and a recreational skydiver. He'd taken enemy fire at the age of eighteen as a soldier during the British invasion of the Falklands, and worked as a nanny-slash-housekeeper in Beverly Hills for a few years in the '90s. After all that, he'd created some of the first real "reality shows" in the world, taking the model of programs like *Cops* and *The Real World* and smashing it together with the drama and tension common in soap operas and action movies. At its root, his story is a good one—an immigrant who comes to the United States with a couple of hundred bucks, then works a few odd jobs until he's got the capital and connections to make his dream come true.

His vision culminated in *Survivor*, an hour-long show that involved contestants stripping off most of their clothing, competing in games, eating gross things, and then getting very mean and voting each other off an island, sort of like the swamp in Washington, DC. Though I doubt Mr. Trump was a fan of the show, he certainly admired the popularity of it and what it did for the producers and stars. But he had no real interest in the show from a business standpoint. People had pitched multicamera shows in which Trump would be shown making deals, eating dinner, and going to meetings. Sort of what *Keeping Up with the Kardashians* is today. He turned them all down summarily, not really understanding the appeal of the medium. I don't blame him. But as with everything else, he remained open to suggestions and pitches.

He remained open that morning in May when Mark Burnett pitched him a show that would take the intensity and confrontational appeal of *Survivor* and transplant it to a New York City boardroom. He didn't say much other than that the show would be "a new jungle reality show, only the jungle would be the concrete one of New York City and the world of big business." Burnett said he had come up with the idea when he'd arrived in America a few years before, and that he'd been waiting for a host who could make it work.

"I knew there was only one master who was colorful enough, charismatic enough," Burnett would recall in the production notes of the DVD.

One week later, they had a meeting in Mr. Trump's office on the twenty-sixth floor of Trump Tower. Burnett filled him in on the details and layout for the show. It would be a thirteen-week job interview, with contestants chosen from across the country, and at the end, the winner would get a six-figure salary and a position running one of Donald Trump's businesses. It was the perfect way to position Mr. Trump as the king of his own castle again, to show him to the world as the man in charge rather than a guy who was continually clawing his way back from the brink of collapse.

Trump agreed to the format, and they began pitching the show to network executives.

As soon as they heard Donald Trump's name, however, most network negotiators said no. They doubted that the show was worth much money, and couldn't see a world in which anyone outside of New York City would care about Donald Trump. People knew his buildings, but they didn't care much about the man himself, was the thinking. (I believe most of those visionaries were later fired but found jobs as pollsters for the 2016 presidential campaign.) *The*

Apprentice, as some people saw, would change all that. In the end, ABC had offered too little money in an attempt to lowball Burnett and Trump, and they were thrown out on their asses early in the process. CBS was interested, too, but they were outgunned during negotiations.

Early in the process, years before he ran CNN, a man by the name of Jeff Zucker decided he wanted the show, and that he'd do anything to get it. His network had built an entire Thursday-night lineup around *Friends*, which would soon be going off the air. If he didn't find a replacement for that show, things would go downhill quickly, and he'd be in danger of losing his new job as the head of all shows for NBC. One night he locked Trump, Mark Burnett, and their representatives in a conference room, and wouldn't let them out until they had renegotiated and signed the contract. Most of the corrections were made in pencil, and there weren't even lawyers present for most of it.

As a TV entertainment exec, Jeff Zucker was a real killer, and he knew how to get things done. Before long, he'd locked down the show for just under $2 million. It premiered in 2004 with a group of contestants who had big-business ambitions and dreams of shaking hands with Donald Trump. They'd been culled from cities around the country based on a lengthy audition process and flown in to record the show at Trump Tower. The fifth floor—which would later become the campaign headquarters during the 2016 campaign for president—became an all-purpose television set, complete with cameras and that dark, moody boardroom you saw on television. Occasionally during the campaign you'd still trip over a camera wire or a piece of sound equipment when you were walking between offices.

The show was a lot of fun. There was a gag that involved selling lemonade on the floor of the New York Stock Exchange, and a "pedicab" challenge that had contestants riding those little half-cab, half-bicycle things around the streets of Manhattan. I thought they seemed pretty funny. But what people really seemed interested in was the end of the show, when Trump would gather everyone in the boardroom, berate them, and then tell someone they were fired. "You're fired" became his catchphrase, which I always found odd. After all, I never actually heard those words from his mouth, and he fired me for real!

It's something that people often get wrong about Mr. Trump, mostly because of the solemn exterior and tough-guy attitude he puts on. He hates firing people himself, and he cares deeply about each one of his employees. I've often said that if he does have one fatal flaw, it's that he's too trusting. In situations where you or I might assume that someone is out to get us or to fight for their own interests, I've found that Donald Trump usually assumes that people have the best of intentions until he's given incontrovertible evidence that they don't. It's what allowed him to trust shady figures like Steve Bannon and Reince Priebus for as long as he did. Where everyone else saw social climbers who were out to suck their own— Ha! Fooled you!—look out for themselves, Donald Trump saw people who just wanted to serve their country. He let them work in the White House until they gave him proof that they didn't have his best interests at heart, then let them go. I joined the White House at a difficult time, and mishandled a situation and was let go, but the president and I have remained friends.

I should note that this isn't a flaw, exactly. It's part of what's allowed him to become so successful. He can see the best in people, even when they've been rejected by the system or counted out by just about everyone already. I know for a fact that he could never have gotten the best deals done on his construction projects if he wasn't willing to overlook a few personal flaws in foremen and contractors over the years. When you're dealing with Donald Trump, the only things that matter are the value you can provide him and how loyal you've been to him in the past. You leave your past screwups and the last few lines on your résumé at the door.

In that sense, at least, *The Apprentice* was a perfect introduction to Donald Trump. It did a good job portraying the meritocratic world in which he operated and continues to operate. It also serves as a perfect metaphor for what a unique personality he has. That is, no one else before or since has been able to make this show work. Not long after *The Apprentice* premiered, Richard Branson tried a similar show, called *The Rebel Billionaire*, which aired on Fox. It tanked after a season. Arnold Schwarzenegger took over for Mr. Trump, and he tanked too. Mark Cuban came up with a show called *The Benefactor*, which didn't even make it through five episodes. Admittedly, Trump had gone after that one personally, saying on Jay Leno's show that Cuban's show would fail. Again, moves like this put Donald Trump's flair for marketing and self-promotion on full display. It was becoming clear that he was far more than just a businessman who had a television show. He was a personification of big business in America, a walking comeback story with a name you couldn't forget. "It's very unusual," Mr. Trump once said about his surname, "but it just is a good name to have." You better believe it. Whereas guys like Richard Branson and Mark Cuban could hold their own on television and promote their products, Mr. Trump made himself into the product, and demand skyrocketed.

By the second episode, *The Apprentice* was a bona fide hit, drawing over 20 million viewers and crushing CBS's ratings champ, *CSI*.

"It was a watershed in self-promotion, coldly and carefully designed as a business strategy to achieve millions in free publicity," said Peter Hauspurg, the chairman of Eastern Consolidated Properties, a several-billion-dollar-a-year commercial real estate firm.

Hauspurg had been asked by a *New York Times* reporter to critique the show.

In just a few years, Mr. Trump had become part of popular culture. I don't know whether you've got any familiarity with rap music, but a quick Google search will tell you that Donald Trump's name has appeared in more rap songs than any modern celebrity in the world. He was on commercials and morning shows and sitting courtside at boxing matches again. He hadn't put his bankruptcy, which he worked into the title sequence of *The Apprentice*, behind him; he made it part of his appeal.

When the original version of *The Apprentice* ended in 2007, Trump began negotiations with the political establishment. They didn't know these negotiations were going on, but he did, and he was making careful calculations that would eventually form into a successful campaign for president.

In 2000, he'd made a half-hearted attempt at a third-party candidacy. In a move that prefigured his campaign in 2016, he'd run on the ticket of the Reform Party, which was formed by people who sensed the oncoming polarization between the Left and the Right in the United States, and he had named Oprah Winfrey as his ideal running mate. But his campaign, like all great populist movements in the history of the United States, came up against the establishment's system early, and it fell apart. Even with a healthy number of votes in the California primaries, he realized it'd be crazy to try to go up against both the Democrats and the Republicans.

To win the presidency, he learned, he'd have to hitch his wagon to one of the country's major parties. Neither one fit him exactly, of course, just like they don't fit me or most of the people in the United States. But it's the way our system is set up, and candidates need to make concessions in order to win. Running for the presidency, in that sense, is not unlike making a deal. You go in with a list full of things you need, knowing all the while that you're going to have to shave a few off the top. You also know there's going to be a percentage of people, a base, for whom you must stay whole. The policies that draw these people are nonnegotiable. These are the core beliefs, and it helps if you believe in them.

There's a story in Jay Winik's book about Reagan, *On the Brink*. It's 1979, and Reagan was reloading to run for president again. The John Birch Society had decided to endorse him, and Reagan aides were losing their minds. And Reagan turned to them and asked why this was such a disaster. They explained that endorsement would pull him too far to the hard right. Reagan turned and asked them who was endorsing whom. The John Birch Society was coming around to his views, not the other way around, he told them. He was sixty-eight at the time. He'd already been a TV star and a movie star, traveled the world, done the General Electric Theater. He'd lived an amazing life, and, like President Trump, wasn't going to change for anyone. If he didn't win because of it, he told his staff, he was going to go to Santa Barbara, go up to his ranch, and cut brush.

Looking back, it's clear. As with most things Donald Trump does, all you have to do is look carefully, and you'll find that his life is not as chaotic as the newspapers make it seem. He knows who he is, what he wants, and how to make it happen.

By 2008, Donald Trump had one of the most recognizable faces in the world.

CHAPTER TEN

SALT

"The mystery of human existence lies not
in just staying alive, but in finding something to live for."
—FYODOR DOSTOYEVSKY,
The Brothers Karamazov

"Don't take any shit from anyone."
—BILLY JOEL

SkyBridge Alternatives Conference. (Scaramucci family collection)

IN FEBRUARY 2009, Barack Obama hosted a town hall meeting in Elkhart, Indiana. He was still relatively new to the office, and he had just put a stimulus package, called the American Recovery and Reinvestment Act of 2009, before Congress. The policy was based on a theory advanced by John Maynard Keynes during the Great Depression. Keynes said that during recessions, the government should offset the decrease in private spending with a sharp increase in public spending—that is, when people and banks get too scared to spend money, the government needs to spend it for them. This was a relatively moderate notion, considering the circumstances. I never got on board with some of my colleagues at Fox who denounced it as socialism.

On the stage in Indiana, Obama gave a good speech on how he planned to get working-class people buying assets again. He would make it easier for people to be approved for loans, and he would inject enough cash and tax breaks to jump start the economy. It was pretty good.

When it was time for questions, a gentleman from one of the surrounding towns got up and told the president how badly he and his friends were hurting. He had had his home foreclosed on, and he wanted to make sure the money from the stimulus package would go to his hometown, not the banks. It was a softball, and he threw it slow and over the plate, saying, "We hope and we pray that you would support the people who got you into office. We the People. Not the fat cats. Send that check to our mailbox!"

There were cheers from the crowd and a wave of recognition all through the stands. You could see heads nodding in the seats behind where Obama was standing. I think he had a chance to stick up for our financial institutions there, but he didn't. It would have been more in line with the moderate platform he ran on. Instead, he played to the audience.

"We're going to make sure the money that goes into Wall Street has some strings attached," he said. "You are not going to be able to give these big bonuses until you pay taxpayers back. You can't get corporate jets. You can't take a trip to Las Vegas or go down to the Super Bowl on the taxpayer's dime. There has got to be some accountability and respectability, and that's something that I intend to impose as president of the United States."

You have to hand it to him; the guy knocked that one out of the park. If he was trying to drum up animosity toward Wall Street in service of getting his legislation passed—which is exactly what he was doing—he couldn't have delivered a better line—no more Vegas for you, Wall Street.

★ �__ ★ �__ ★

MANY, MANY INNOCENT, everyday Americans were hurt by the banking crisis. My father lost a third of his retirement fund, and there were plenty hurt worse than he was. So to try to defend the financial community from back in that time might seem tone deaf. Not everyone in Wall Street, however, was responsible for the crash. Believe it or not, many of us were victims of it too.

During one of the low points of the crisis, in the early months of 2009, I bought a plastic mouthpiece for my teeth. I had been grinding them pretty hard at night—the sound of it would wake me up. Even in my sleep, it seemed, I was back at the office, poring over the books and having visions of my company's demise.

In the preceding months, I had watched employees at Lehman Brothers, many of whom were my friends, leaving the bank's Manhattan headquarters in droves. They were like zombies. Most of them carried cardboard boxes full of their things, ducking to avoid television cameras. With the help of the United States Treasury, J.P. Morgan had bought Bear Stearns. The government had taken control of Fannie Mae and Freddie Mac. Wachovia, Bank of America, and other well-known banks were hanging on for dear life. Things on my side of the street weren't looking much better. Hedge funds much bigger than my own, with double and triple the staff and fifty times the assets, had closed up shop for good. Nearly everyone I spoke with told me I was next. Any day, they said, I was going to follow the bankers of Lehman up to that big, sad executive suite in the sky.

So yeah, I was grinding my teeth.

AT THE TIME, I was running SkyBridge Capital. In 2005, right after I left Lehman, along with Andrew Klein, who had made a fortune underwriting Internet stocks, I helped found SkyBridge as sort of a hedge fund's hedge fund (I would buy Andy out two years later). We helped money managers who wanted to go out on their own with seeding capital. An incubator. It was a good idea, and the business started strong. Michael Dell invested in the firm, and the stock markets were streaking upward. It was like that old disco song "Everybody Dance." The music, however, wouldn't last. By late 2007, the financial world had begun to tremble from the coming subprime mortgage crisis. By 2008, it was Looney Tunes. I felt like Wile E. Coyote just after he'd run off a cliff, churning his feet, nothing below but air. I was working twenty-hour days, existing on adrenaline and fear. I'd go home, collapse, and the alarm would go off—or that's how it seemed. One summer during law school, I took a Dale Carnegie course and read Carnegie's book *How to Stop Worrying and Start Living.* I believe firmly in Carnegie's philosophy, but it was going to take more than one summer class about it to help me though the situation I was in.

W HEN YOU'RE FIGHTING for the survival of your business, things become so overwhelming the rest of your life fades out of view. I was forty-four, with three kids in school. I didn't have time for them or anyone else. I had to save the ship or we all would sink.

One night in early October, David called me at my office. My brother's relapse had taken me by surprise. He had started going to bars again, drinking ginger ale, playing darts, just to shoot the shit, he said. Harmless stuff. There's a saying in AA, however, that goes something like: if you hang around a barbershop long enough, you're going to get a haircut. He began cutting back on AA meetings. He told us that his life was fine, that he didn't need them. On the outside, his life looked that way. But addicts and alcoholics are deft at keeping trouble to themselves until they can't. One night David went out with a bunch of Wall Street guys, including a younger dude whom David didn't know. The kid had a gram of coke on him, and when he offered some to my brother, David didn't even think twice. Poof! Just like that. Nine years of sobriety down the drain. That one line of coke was like a key to a cage that held the demon. Once that cage was opened, the beast had my brother by the throat.

In the AA program, they call relapse a "slip" or "going out." Those phrases don't exactly capture the seriousness of the event. An alcoholic or drug addict who relapses, especially after a long period of sobriety, can cause an enormous amount of damage to himself and those around him, especially to those who love them. Trust built up over the first length of sobriety is obliterated. In one way, David was lucky. He was "out" for only nine months or so, and he didn't lose his job or completely wreck his marriage. It could have been much worse.

Mr. Trump and I would later talk about addiction often during the campaign. We both have experience with it. Like David, like many alcoholics I'm told, Mr. Trump's brother, Fred Trump Jr., had a dynamic personality and was loved by everyone. Similar to my relationship with David, Mr. Trump idolized his older brother. Handsome and daring, Fred was an airline pilot for TWA by his early twenties. His alcoholism made quick work of him, however; he was only forty-three when he died of the disease—nearly the same age my brother was when he went out on his slip.

I knew why David was calling. He was celebrating his one-year anniversary at his AA home group in Port Washington, and he wanted me there. I knew there was no chance I would be able to make it. I let the call go to voicemail.

It was close to eleven o'clock at night by the time I left the office and headed for Port Washington. The train was nearly empty. People were chatting, sipping beer from clear plastic cups, and falling asleep while leaning against the windows and missing their stops. The seats in front of me were filled with tired stockbrokers and bankers, still wearing suits and ties that hung loose around their necks like little nooses. You could practically feel the desperation.

I knew these were the people that the country would blame for everything. Within months, anyone with a job that bore even a tangential connection to Wall Street would be vilified and demonized. The papers and the government would point one collective finger in the direction of the banks, and public anger would follow. No one would talk about all the good the financial sector had done for the world—how it had provided the capital and encouragement to small businesses, fueling the longest sustained period of economic growth in all of human history, how it had built Main Street from nothing. They would only see the failure. They would need someone to blame, and Wall Street would seem the easy choice. Not that it would be entirely undeserved.

It was investment bankers on Wall Street, after all, who invented something called the mortgage-backed security in the early 1970s—a product, as you might recall, that became the cause of the financial crisis. These securities (a fancy word for stocks and bonds) were built by bankers and signed off on by lawyers. Bankers would buy up mortgages from local banks all around the country, bundle them together in groups of a few thousand each, and then sell the whole collection the way you'd sell stocks. The logic was that people rarely default on their mortgages, so the securities would always be worth something. They would only increase in value. This made them popular among individual retirement accounts and pension funds. My own father's retirement account, for example, contained a whole lot of money that was linked to this kind of security.

He and the other guys at Gotham Sand and Stone, unfortunately, would lose a third of their pension fund. Stories like his and even more were replicated millions of times across the country.

The official narrative of the crisis says that when some mortgage-backed security traders—who represented about 1 percent of all the people who work on Wall Street—started including bad mortgages in their bundles without telling investors, they knowingly laid the groundwork for collapse. These bankers, so the story goes, chopped up the mortgage-backed securities and created things called collateralized debt obligations, weak asset-backed securities that became worthless when the housing market collapsed. Then, when the whole thing came crashing down, and they were left holding billions of dollars in bad assets, they had the taxpayers foot the bill, as the bankers knew they would have to.

They were getting bankrolled by Main Street to play high-stakes poker, then going for broke on every hand.

But it's rarely mentioned that the actual roots of the financial crisis can be found in Washington—not Wall Street. As far back as the Clinton administration, the federal government made home ownership a priority. Early in 2002, when George W. Bush was first laying out plans to build what he called his Ownership Society—a program, he said, under which home ownership would increase, the tax code would be revamped, health care would be privatized, and Social Security would be revolutionized—the Federal Reserve lowered interest rates to around 1 percent. This sudden drop, which came on the heels of a massive budget surplus, was meant to send a message to the American public that it was safe to take on big mortgages—even ones with payments they wouldn't typically be able to afford. The Bush administration envisioned a world in which all Americans could own homes and enjoy the dignity and prosperity that came with home ownership. It was a lofty goal, but it didn't come along with any discussion of responsibility or viability, which would be its downfall.

By 2005, home ownership was the only portion of the Ownership Society that was still viable. Congress had refused to touch Social Security, health care, or the tax code, fearing the political ramifications if they tried. By the fall of 2005, the home ownership rate in the United States reached 69 percent, and many of those homes were financed with faulty mortgages and other bank loans. Local banks had taken the government's lead and started offering mortgages with no down payments and no income requirement. Virtually anyone—regardless of credit rating, amount of collateral, or ability to pay—could secure a mortgage and buy a house. Still, the faulty thinking went: if homeownership in the United States was up, politicians would have something to run on. Bush figured it would help get him reelected, which it did (along with the promise to keep us safe from terrorists). But he and the members of Congress who helped him pass legislation on housing didn't see what was going on with the actual people who were buying these homes—just like they didn't see factory jobs being moved overseas or immigrants pouring illegally over the border in droves.

Some things about the Swamp, as you'll see, never change.

They didn't see that people in the working and middle classes of America were digging themselves into a massive hole, or that the mortgages they'd been encouraged to buy were destined to fail. Only when the mortgages failed—when millions of people stopped paying and slipped into default, as Washington should have known they would—did the collapse happen. Investment banks on Wall Street, which had bought up the mortgages, were left holding billions of dollars in bad debt, and they had no one left to sell them to. Within months, the government was cleaning up a mess it had played an enormous part in making, shaking its finger all the while at the closest thing it could find: Wall Street. Hedge funds. Bankers. Anyone who wore a suit to work and traded stocks for a living. In short: me and my colleagues, most of whom wouldn't know a mortgage-backed security if one smacked them in the face.

As I looked around the train that night, I was sure no one else on it knew much about them, either. But I also knew that many of them were fighting to stay alive just like I was, and even though they had nothing to do with the banking collapse.

I thought of the struggle that bankers had endured for decades after the Great Depression, how long it had taken for them to get back in the good graces of the public so they could start trading and guiding the economy again. I hoped the same kind of drought wasn't about to happen but felt that it might be. If the government started making people feel like Wall Street was the enemy of small business, it would mean slow growth and pain for everyone. I didn't want to let that happen. There were too many important things to invent and build; too much of the country was bound up in the success of Wall Street to pit it against Main Street for political purposes. It was clear, however, that exactly that was about to happen, at least for a little while.

As the train moved through Jamaica Station in Queens, past the Trump Pavilion at the Jamaica Hospital and the streaming head-lights of the Long Island Expressway, I thought that I was on the verge of losing control. I thought of my brother again. It felt as if I was in the middle of one of the novels by Philip Roth or Thomas Mann that I'd loved in college—living out a personal crisis while a parallel political one unfolded around me. My business, into which I had sunk nearly every penny, was entering what I thought was a death spiral. The economy of the United States was collapsing; the pension fund my father had worked forty years at Gotham Sand and Stone to build was getting cut by more than a third, and home val-ues in the neighborhood I grew up in and loved were sinking. I was spending more time at the office than ever while my children grew up without me, and I had no idea whether that office would still be there in a week. And through it all, my brother was in a daily battle to resist the pull of drugs and alcohol and had succeeded in that bat-tle for a whole year.

It was almost midnight by the time the train pulled into Port Washington. David's AA celebration had been over for hours. There was a light burning inside when I pulled into his driveway. He opened the door when I knocked. I think back on that moment, and

I wonder how it must have looked. I was the one who looked like shit, and David, with eyes that shone with one year's sobriety, looked like a million bucks. We stood and hugged in the doorframe. He said he was sorry for all he had done to me. I told him I was sorry for missing the meeting and then began to talk about how lousy business was.

"Bro," he said. "I'm just grateful to have people around me who love me. The rest of it doesn't matter."

I now wish I could have felt the way David did back then—lucky to be alive and surrounded by people who loved me. I thought my world would crack and fall to pieces if SkyBridge failed, and that image kept me from seeing anything else.

ONE YEAR PASSED, and my business didn't go under. It felt like a miracle, but it wasn't. I had just surrounded myself with a good team who always kept their heads on straight, even when mine began spinning out of control. But the mood on Wall Street was still somber. No one wanted to innovate or make big plays. I was still grinding my teeth at night.

We were staying alive, but barely. We had fought with everything we had.

Then came President Barack Obama's town hall meeting and statement: "We're going to make sure the money that goes into Wall Street has some strings attached... You can't take a trip to Las Vegas or go down to the Super Bowl on the taxpayer's dime."

I knew that he was trying to drum up support for a stimulus package, which passed a few days after his speech, and that package turned out to be a good thing. It flooded the market with liquidity and encouraged investment in the stock market. The Federal Reserve also lowered interest rates from 6 percent to just above 0.

This was necessary to get people spending money again. There was more liquidity in the markets than there had been in years. But his remark was a broad brush that painted every corner of Wall Street as untrustworthy and underhanded. Along with directing more ire toward the financial sector than there already was, it brought networking on Wall Street almost to a stop.

Nobody on the Street wanted to take a chance. People only wanted to keep their heads down, far away from the big bad government. That year every bank in the country canceled their conferences—which were events, usually held in places like Las Vegas, that were designed to inspire innovation and foster connections within the financial sector—and encouraged their employees to stay away too. There was a culture of silence and sullenness on Wall Street. People were afraid to speak, afraid even to make the big, bold deals they used to make. Even individual bankers were encouraged to stay out of the spotlight. One wrong move could mean a month of public shaming.

Something had to be done.

Like the rest of us, Victor Oviedo, my partner at SkyBridge, had watched all the somber faces as he walked to work each morning, and had felt the desperation among people on the Street. These were not the faces of people who were ready to bring the American economy back from the brink of collapse, he told me. They were the faces of people who were prepared to take their beating from Obama and say, "Thank you, sir," when it was over. This wasn't who we were.

There's a moment in all stories on which the outcome depends. This was one of them. If Victor hadn't said what he did to me sometime after Obama's remark, chances are our hedge fund wouldn't have become the success it's become. It's also possible that it might have taken Wall Street much longer to grow back its balls. It's practically a certainty that I would have never become the White House communications director. Of course, I had no idea that Victor's words held such importance. In looking back, though, I can tell you they were about as perfect as words can get.

"How 'bout we go to Vegas?" he said with a smile.

WHEN VICTOR TOLD me about his idea to hold a hedge fund networking event in Sin City, I thought he'd lost his mind. After only a few moments, though, I began to see the brilliance in the idea. Thanks to comments like Obama's, people were going to think we were entitled, rich assholes who blew the public's money in Vegas regardless if we went there or not. So there was a minimal downside. The upside was we might be able make connections, even cut deals, which might inject a little life into the cadaver of the hedge fund industry. Plus, and this was a big plus, we might bring back a little pride to the whole financial sector. I had friends in those days who were afraid even to say they worked on Wall Street. Some people would boo you just for wearing a suit and walking into a hedge fund office every morning.

That had to end.

After a few conversations with Victor, I called Oscar Goodman, the mayor of Las Vegas, and told him I wanted to bring a hedge fund conference to his city. Obama had cost him a few million dollars in tax revenue, so he was more than happy to oblige. I also got in touch with the Wall Street icon Michael Milken, who'd always been a hero of mine, and Steve Wynn, whose Encore Hotel we wanted to host the event. I didn't know what to expect when I called Milken—I thought he might just hang up on me. He didn't.

"Sure," he said.

Steve Wynn was just as easy. The only thing left to do was talk the rest of our team into it.

SALT

About two months before the scheduled date for the conference, in March of 2009, Victor and I called all five of the other SkyBridge partners into our conference room for a vote. I thought I would pitch the idea, address a few minor concerns, ask for a vote, and count the yeses. In hindsight, I might have been a bit cocky. You have to remember: we still weren't sure we'd make it through the day, let alone survive to throw a bash in Vegas.

When I pitched the idea, their response was, well, less than enthusiastic. You would have thought I was asking them to donate a kidney.

"What's the worst that can happen?" I asked, trying to add a little levity.

"At least we'll have a going-out-of-business party!"

When it came time for the vote, Victor and I were the only ones who were for the idea. 5–2.

There's an old story about Abraham Lincoln that I've always liked, although it's probably apocryphal. It tells of a cabinet meeting he held just after he'd drafted the Emancipation Proclamation, when he wanted the nine members of his cabinet to vote on it. When they did, all nine of them said no. Lincoln was the only aye. "Nine nays and one aye," Lincoln said, raising his right hand. "The ayes have it."

As the co-founder of SkyBridge, I decided on a similar approach.

"Gentlemen, I hear your concerns," I said. "Thank you for voting. We're doing it anyway."

Before I knew it, we were boarding planes for Vegas and hoping our fund would still be running when we got back. We decided to call the conference SALT, short for SkyBridge Alternatives. We had booked a few businesses, so I knew the conference wouldn't be a total bust, but I wasn't sure how the thing would go once we touched down in Nevada. When the lights finally went up, and Steve Wynn introduced me to the crowd of about five hundred as Andy

Scaramucci, I took it as a good omen. It was. Steve Wynn getting my name wrong was the only hiccup all weekend. People met on casino floors and walked together along the Vegas Strip, many of them laughing for the first time in months. We heard speakers who'd come up with wild ideas for breathing new life into the market but were too afraid to mention them in the boardrooms back home, and people from all corners of the investing world who had come looking for support and found it. More connections and deals came out of that weekend than had been made in weeks back in New York. What made me most proud, however, was the atmosphere we'd been able to create—a place where people who were being shunned and derided in the outside world could come and be themselves and proud of what they did again. We had shown the politicians and reporters that we weren't going to take any shit from anyone, and they responded by either shutting up or getting on board.

As the conference was winding down, Steve Wynn pulled me aside.

"Thanks for helping Vegas," he said. "What the president didn't know was how many middle-class people depend on events like this: bellhops, maids, waitstaff, taxi drivers, and a dozen other jobs."

Wall Street seemed a little different when we returned to New York. Maybe I only imagined it, but I could feel a renewed sense of purpose, as if a thick storm cloud had finally drifted away. Everyone could move again. This didn't happen all at once, and I'm not sure how much of it was SkyBridge and how much was simply the passage of time. Still, more than once—much more—people from the Street came up to me and Victor to thank us for SALT, and for making them feel good about what they did for a living again. Maybe it didn't amount to what my brother was doing on Long Island, helping drug addicts and alcoholics find a life again, but it wasn't bad. In the aftermath of the SALT conference, I felt we were no longer just fighting to stay alive. We had something to stay alive for.

B Y THE NEXT YEAR, I had secured Bill Clinton as a keynote speaker, and we had to start turning people away. We capped the attendance levels at 1,400, which was still massive for a hotel conference. I didn't mind. Large parties are often nice and intimate, as Jordan Baker says in *The Great Gatsby*. At small parties, there isn't any privacy.

That year, we helped facilitate more deals at the conference than the year before, and the press began to love it. The presence of a former president of the United States, who spoke at length about negotiations with North Korea, didn't do any harm to that love affair with the press. Just before he attended the SALT conference, Bill Clinton had flown to Pyongyang to negotiate the release of four political prisoners held by North Korea—something Donald Trump would do a few years later over the phone, by the way—and he spoke about the threat that country would continue to pose in the future. Funny how any type of peace deal with North Korea seemed so far away not so long ago. Clinton's appearance, though, elevated SkyBridge from a small meeting of hedge funds to a place where leaders of all kinds could meet and connect with one another.

Over the coming years, we would book former presidents, movie and sports stars, and titans of business and finance. Before I knew it, I had become the public face of SkyBridge and SALT. Reporters were doing profiles of me, painting me as some Gatsby-esque figure who threw wild parties out in the desert. I took a lesson from Donald J. Trump and let them print what they wanted. When you're in a tight spot, it always helps to cultivate a good image of yourself.

However, you have to learn early with the media that you aren't going to be able to control the complete narrative. Repetition will eventually paint the full picture, but let's face it, the media is looking to sketch a caricature. Before long, SALT was a massive hit—"a self-styled Davos meets *Wolf of Wall Street* that attracts top names from Hollywood, sports and politics," according to *Politico*. It became a forum for Democrats and Republicans to come together and discuss their differences outside of Washington and all the nonsense that comes with that place. For a while, it was a paradise in the sand—at least for a few years.

But a strong economy, which eventually came as a result of renewed faith in Wall Street, is nothing if the government is still pushing dangerous policies like the ones that caused the financial crisis. If people in the White House don't care about what's going on with the aspirational working class in America—the people who hold no assets and weren't helped much by the Obama stimulus package—we're doomed to repeat our failures. All the cool conferences in the world can't replace a good president who understands the working class and Wall Street at the same time.

I STARTED THIS CHAPTER with a story about an Obama town hall meeting, and I'm going to end it with one. In this one, however, yours truly played a starring role, and the outcome wasn't quite as rosy. As a result of my experience with SALT, I was as confident as a wolf in front of the camera. I did media hits constantly on financial and news channels. I was one of the only recognizable hedge fund people on TV. No matter how big of a wolf you are, however, if you're not careful TV can turn around and bite you.

The day started off great. Oliver Stone's sequel to *Wall Street*, the movie *Wall Street: Money Never Sleeps*, was having a premiere at the

Ziegfeld Theatre in Manhattan. Stone had asked me to be in the film a few years earlier. If you fast-forward a few minutes into that movie, you can see me talking on the phone during a transition shot, demanding a piece of some stock. Nobody's gonna compare me to Al Pacino, but it was fun. Just before the premiere, CNBC called and asked if I would participate in the town hall meeting that they were televising that afternoon. These televised town hall events might seem spontaneous, but they're not. Everything is scripted and choreographed. I was to be one of six audience members to ask the president a question. I was to represent Wall Street. At this point, the anti–Wall Street sentiment still ran strong, especially among Obama's faithful. I might have let my ego get in the way of good sense. It happens. With my question, I defended Wall Street but posed it in a way that left me wide open. The president didn't like the question at all, and took advantage.

That night, after the event, I got a call from my son, AJ, who was then a sophomore at Tufts University.

"Dad," he said excitedly. "Turn on Comedy Central."

Among other things, I had asked the president when he was going to stop whacking the Wall Street piñata. In so many words, he responded that it wasn't Wall Street but Main Street that was taking the beating. The crowd applauded, and I sat down.

The Daily Show's Jon Stewart introduced the clip by calling me a "Jersey Shore breakout star," and it only got worse from there. My choice of metaphor might not have been the best. When you look like me and have a Mafia-boss-sounding last name like Scaramucci, it's probably not wise to talk about whacking anything on television. Stewart ate my lunch. The truth is, I threw Obama an alley-oop, and he flushed it, as he should have. It was his show. But Obama's performance that night also displayed what I think is the fundamental problem with politics in our country. For too long, we've been letting politicians in Washington pit small business against investment banking, the flower shop on the corner against the fund manager in a corner office, when in reality those people need to work together if they want to prosper.

I think what bothered me the most about that night was an internet screed I read. The post called me an out-of-touch Wall Street elitist. Screw you, I thought. I'd pulled myself up by the bootstraps and worked like a dog for everything I had. The truth was, however, that that's exactly what I'd become. The rocket I was on had burst through the atmosphere, and what came next vaulted me further into the upper-crust establishment and farther away from the forgotten America on the ground.

CHAPTER ELEVEN

OUR PATHS CONVERGE

President George W. Bush spoke at one of the SALT conferences. He called me "Gucci Scaramucci"! (Scaramucci family collection)

THE FIRST TIME I met Donald Trump I was thirty-two, and I was awestruck. At that age, I hadn't met many famous people, and he was about as famous as you could get, at least for a kid growing up in the New York City area. I had read *The Art of the Deal*, and it had had a significant impact on me. For a blue-collar guy, working in finance, who wanted to rise through the economic classes and reach for the Gold Ring, Mr. Trump was the Great Gatsby.

I met him at his office in Trump Tower with Mike Fascitelli, my old boss. Mike was then the president of Vornado Realty Trust, a building developer and management company, and he and Mr. Trump were meeting about a joint venture deal. I had just started Oscar Capital, a hedge fund, and was looking for investors. Mike invited me along.

Mr. Trump was seated at his desk, that jaw-dropping view of Central Park behind him. I was nervous. I'm very outgoing, and sometimes that can work against me when I meet people for the first time. I remember trying to keep myself in check, trying not to come on too strong. Mr. Trump didn't invest in my fund, but he was gracious and funny, and I distinctly remember thinking that he wasn't at all like the image, the out-of-touch billionaire in a gilded tower, the press had concocted of him.

Over the next few years, as my fortunes rose, I would run into

Mr. Trump at charity events such as the Robin Hood fund-raising dinner. Robin Hood is a New York charity that fights poverty, partly by paying the rent for people who have lost their ability to support themselves. I reintroduced myself the first time I ran into him, but after that, I didn't have to. I always called him "Mr. Trump," and he appreciated that. Donald Trump is an ageist. By that, I mean that he believes seniority has its privileges. He'll take bullshit from Carl Icahn. Icahn's ten years older, and he's worth billions of dollars. He'll talk laterally to Steve Schwarzman; he's in his peer group. But if you're Steven Mnuchin or Anthony Scaramucci, or anyone else who's younger than he, you had better be deferential.

For some reason, the clearest image of him I have from those years has him in an overcoat. Just like the ones he wears now. Even at baseball games, he'd wear it. On Mitt Romney's campaign, I'd become friendly with Woody Johnson, and through Woody, I met Randy Levine, the president of the Yankees. We'd all go together to Yankee Stadium and watch the game from George Steinbrenner's box. It seemed like Mr. Trump was always there, talking with Reggie Jackson, Yogi Berra, or Regis Philbin and, with that overcoat, looked as though he had another stop to make.

One day, I was at a Lupus Foundation luncheon fund-raiser hosted by the New York Jets where I was seated right next to Donald Trump. I wasn't in the best of moods that day. A writer from Reuters had published a critical article about a wine gathering I'd hosted. Among other things, he called me a snob and an elitist, and referred to my guests as drunks. Considering all that's happened to me since, that story from long ago seems tame. Back then, however, it bothered me. Mr. Trump noticed my mood and asked me what the matter was. I told him the story.

"Look," he said, "it comes with the territory. First of all, it means you're big stuff now. They don't shoot at the small fries. Second of all, you can't let it get to you. They've been writing hit pieces on me for thirty years. The sooner you build up a resistance, the better."

Can you imagine getting that kind of advice from Donald Trump? Like Leonardo da Vinci teaching you how to paint by numbers.

MY FIRST REAL foray into politics was a sort of a crazy, impulsive episode for which, as I once told Charles and David Koch, I've been doing penance to the Republican Party ever since. Up until then, my interaction with politicians was typical of a New York businessperson, meaning, hypothetically, if a client came to me and said, "I'm doing a fund-raiser for Mitch McConnell, would you write a $1,000 check?" my answer would be yes. If another client called me two minutes later and said, "I'm doing a fund-raiser for a guy named Chuck Schumer, would you write me a check?" I'd say yes. If you look it up, you'll find that I donated to people like Hillary Clinton in the year 2000, when she ran for Senate. You'll also see me giving to Republicans, which was my political choice. In business, however, you don't donate because of affiliation. You donate to help your business.

As far as my politics went as a citizen, I would say I was a center-right person—socially inclusive and fiscally responsible. (I never say "socially liberal and fiscally conservative" because we've spent billions of dollars destroying the words "liberal" and "conservative." The minute you say you're one, the people on the other side hate you.) My political profile, as it turned out, was a much more difficult position to hold than I ever thought it would be. Over my years working with establishment candidates, I found that if you subscribed to one of their positions, you had to accept every single other one without debate. This bulk sales approach, I believe, has stripped voters of the nuance and deep conversation entitled by the

Constitution, and often makes people choose between two wildly different extremes. It didn't bother me yet that most of these positions were decided in the headquarters of the Republican National Committee, but it would very soon.

★ ∕ ★ ∕ ★

BECAUSE I ACTED impulsively, I found myself early in the summer of 2007 standing at a bar with a few guys from my law school class. We had gathered at the University Club in New York City, which, if you've never been, you can imagine as a place where old WASPs covered up their affairs or selected the next governor over single malt scotch and Cohiba cigars. There were leather-bound books on the walls, large wingback chairs, and more old, crusty Ivy League men than you could shake an ascot at. If you've ever seen the movie *Trading Places* with Eddie Murphy and Dan Aykroyd, you have a pretty good idea of how the place looks.

That day, however, there was more vigor than usual in the smoky back room of the University Club. A man named Barack Obama, then the junior senator from Illinois and a favored candidate for president of the United States, was standing at the center of the room holding court, shaking hands, and taking big donation checks. Obama had gone to my law school, and our time at Harvard had briefly overlapped. (He was a first-year law student when I was in my senior year.) I have law school classmates who were close to him and tell me that I played basketball with the future president in the Hemenway Gymnasium. I'll take their word for it. I don't remember. I didn't know Obama in school.

Obama is an engaging guy and, of course, an unparalleled orator. In my mind, I saw him as a moderate with enough business sense to get me, if not fired up, at least on board with his candidacy. His grandstanding on the floor of the Senate about legislation on torture only made me respect him more.

So when I heard that he was considering a run for the presidency, I agreed to bundle for him. In political speak, bundling means calling up your buddies and asking them to donate big piles of money to his campaign, which I did. As a result of the money I raised, I got an invitation to the speech at the University Club. At the time, I was feeling more comfortable than ever at upper-crusty parties like this one, surrounded by people who all thought roughly the same way about politics, and often complained together about their coastal, big-money problems. *Shall I go with the Doric or Corinthian columns for the summer home, Mortimer? What, may I ask, is the name of your helicopter salesman, Randolph?* I accepted the invitation and attended a small gathering in the afternoon, which began a few hours before the speech. The turnout was excellent, and Senator Obama was doing one hell of a job with the crowd. He stood center stage in shirtsleeves and spoke without notes about a whole range of issues. I was impressed.

A few minutes in, I got the chance to shake his hand and talk with him one-on-one. I mentioned that I was about to write him a pretty big check and that some of my friends thought it was kind of a big deal that I had gone to school with someone who might be president. We talked about standard political stuff for a while and touched briefly on the long campaign he had ahead of him. Finally, I said, "Look, I know we weren't all that close in law school, but if I write this check, could I tell people we were really good friends?"

"Sure," he said. "And if you double the size of the check, we can take it all the way back to Hawaii!"

That was one of the last interactions I would have with Barack Obama before the infamous CNBC town hall event in which, as president, he slam-dunked me in front of a live television audience. I should have remembered how quick-witted he was before I lobbed him the piñata question about him beating up on Wall Street. But even after he flushed me, I remained very impressed by the man and all that he was able to accomplish. I've often said he's the Jackie Robinson of American politics, and no one's ever going to take that away from him. Unfortunately, by the time he got to the Oval Office, just about every antibusiness Democrat in the country had gotten their hooks into him. The policies he sought to enact as president were a disaster for Wall Street. Unmitigated disaster. His foreign policy strategy was just as bad.

BY THE NEXT presidential election cycle, I had come to my senses. Obama was championing the rhetoric of people like Elizabeth Warren, whom I find to be a very misguided socialist, and pandering to the Bernie Sanders wing of the Left too often for my taste. And it wasn't only his words. He pushed huge, sweeping legislation such as the Affordable Care Act and the Dodd–Frank Act that not only hurt business but vilified it. Yes, as the campaign for Obama's second term approached, the cloud of the subprime banking crisis still hung over Wall Street. Hedge funds and financial firms were still the bad guys and easy targets. Thanks to a blindly rabid press and hypocritical, liberal Hollywood, public sentiment was still overwhelmingly negative toward Wall Street and the financial industry. Pandering for votes, the president rode the wave instead of trying to help.

By February 2011, having nothing to do with the full facial slam dunk on me at the CNBC town hall event, I'd had enough with Obama. I decided to support a candidate who I thought could challenge him. I was interested in staying involved in politics because I figured the Republicans were going to win eventually and I thought I could be someone who could help influence business policy. That made all the sense in the world, and I had thought I found the perfect guy.

There was a lot to like about Mitt Romney. His economic policies were not so different from the ones espoused by the White House today. Romney wanted to eliminate many of the Obama-era regulations, issue new oil- and gas-drilling permits, and cut the corporate income-tax rate from 35 percent to 25 percent. (President Trump's plan brought it down to 21 percent.) He had perfect hair and an even temper, and he was a God-fearing, morally pristine family man. He was also a walking symbol of Wall Street, which, given the timing of his run, might not have been the best look.

At the time, I was attending political fund-raisers and would often see Romney. At one of these, I mentioned that I had read his book *No Apology* and liked what he had to say. Then I asked him to speak at the second annual SkyBridge SALT Conference, as a kind of Republican counterbalance. That year, I had unknowingly brought together two opposing ends of the US political establishment—people who, presumably, meant well but cared too much about what people thought of them to have any effect at all. Both had decided when they were virtually in diapers that they were going to be president of the United States, and they had lived their entire lives according to that goal. This quest turned them into weathervanes, apt to rotate 180 degrees with any slight change in the political winds. But I thought one of them was my guy, so I wrote him a few checks and spent some time talking strategy with his people.

Except for the Obama aberration, I still viewed politics through a business prism. I took a big step toward partisanship when I agreed to work for Mitt's 2012 presidential campaign. I thought his campaign strategy was well thought out and well executed.

I was able to learn quite a bit, and also have some fun, while I worked with Matt Rhodes, Romney's campaign manager, who was a pro. All along, polling suggested the race was tight, and as the election neared, things were leaning Romney's way. We were hosting expensive dinners and rubbing shoulders with most of the country's wealthiest people, all the while raking in hundreds of thousands of dollars for the candidate every night. Looking back, we didn't spend nearly enough time talking to the working men and women of the United States—the people who'd been left struggling to get by because of the uneven trade deals and the degradation of the American worker that characterized much of the late twentieth century. No one, it turns out, was talking to them. No one would until the next election cycle.

So it was fitting, in a sense, that the whole Romney campaign was nearly brought down by a bartender at a catering company in Boca. The guy had been pouring wine and champagne for rich people at one of our fund-raisers all night, each of whom had paid $50,000 for a seat at the table. Then our mixologist friend decided to prop up his iPhone against a bottle of chardonnay and tap record, perhaps to have a keepsake or to impress his friends. Just as he did, however, Mitt told the room filled with spray-tanned and Botoxed millionaires that 47 percent of the country were tax deadbeats sucking on the welfare teat. He said they would always vote for Obama because they believed the government "had a responsibility to care for them" and that they felt entitled to health care, housing, and food. The moment illustrated the power of social media in politics perhaps for the first time, at least on the presidential-campaign level. For a while the recording looked like a mortal wound for the Romney campaign.

CNN had a field day. They played the video incessantly. Along with the rest of the media, the cable news network made it seem like Romney had only African American and Hispanic families in mind when he said this—playing up the racial divisions and PC debates that always get them eyeballs. They painted him as insensitive and racist, which he isn't, and intimated that he was tone-deaf to the realities of working-class life in the United States—which he kinda was. Mitt's a wonderful guy, but he's lived his whole life around prominent businesspeople and influential politicians who never had to punch a clock or carry a lunch pail to work, so he was less able to recognize the resentment that was brewing among the people that globalization and progressivism had left behind. The aspirational working class of my father's generation had become the desperational working class, and no one in 2012 was listening to their calls for help.

Still, in spite of the 47 percent gaffe, I thought Mitt still had a good chance of winning. As it would turn out, the real difference between the candidates was not the 47 percent remark but Obama's ground game and his campaign's use of databases to microtarget voters. That technique in Obama's hands was heralded as brilliant, but four years later when used in Mr. Trump's campaign, it was called suspicious and part of an international spy-ring plot.

For election night, I'd booked a room at the Westin Hotel next to the Boston Convention and Exhibition Center. I waited for the results at the convention hall with a man named Donald J. Trump. I don't know whether Mr. Trump was feeling the urge to address some of the issues that Romney wasn't, whether he was paying attention to the coal miners and steelworkers in Appalachia or the rampant political correctness on college campuses, but I know he didn't talk about it that night. He only wanted to see Obama out of office, and someone in the White House who would stand up for businesses over government. He'd already been making some pretty aggresive videos from his office in Trump Tower, which I found compelling if a little over the top.

That night, he was tense. In a sense, part of his reputation was on the line. Mr. Trump had endorsed Romney and done some rob-ocalls for him during the primaries and toward the end of the campaign. He had also participated in a fund-raising telethon. Before he backed Mitt, Mr. Trump had debated running himself. He told me, however, that he liked Romney's agenda and thought the timing wasn't right for his run at the presidency. But when a shell-shocked Mitt Romney conceded from the Convention Center's stage, Mr. Trump threw up his hands.

"I made a mistake," he said with disgust. "I should have run."

Before I could say anything to him or ask whether he would run in the future, he had that overcoat of his on and was headed to board his plane for New York.

CHAPTER TWELVE

D-DAY

Taken when I began working for Governor
Scott Walker. My sister Susan and our mom
are with me. (Scaramucci family collection)

Candidate Trump at the rally in Albuquerque, New Mexico. (Kena Betan-
cur AFP / Getty Images)

IT WAS THREE years later, in February of 2015, when I received the call from Rhona Graff, Donald Trump's personal assistant. She told me her boss wanted to see me. She didn't say why, but I took the meeting without asking. By then, I had been friends with Donald Trump for over a decade. I knew that when he wanted to see you it was usually a good idea to take the meeting for many reasons, not the least of which was that the man was never boring.

The following day, February 17, 2015, I was in Mr. Trump's office on the twenty-sixth floor of Trump Tower in Manhattan. He was sitting behind his desk, that same spectacular view of Central Park behind him, all the newspapers and magazines spread out in front of him. By then, Mr. Trump had starred on *The Apprentice* and *Celebrity Apprentice* for fourteen seasons. The show was still going strong, with no end in sight. I didn't have any reason to think he wanted to do anything else. Why would he? The show was a brand machine.

I was wrong.

"I'm running for president," he said to me matter-of-factly, as if we were out to dinner and had decided on the veal scaloppini.

"No, you're not," I said. "Look at the Fox News poll. You're at 2 percent!"

"I know, I know. But it's because people are just like you, Anthony. They don't think I'm running for president."

"I've been in your apartment," I said. "You've got nineteen thousand square feet. The White House living quarters are five thousand square feet! I've been on your plane! Trump Force One is gorgeous, and you're going to ride around with a plane filled with press on Air Force One? Come on; you're not running for president."

Mr. Trump, however, was dead set on the scaloppini.

"No, no, no, the country's gotta get fixed. I'm just the guy to fix it. I hired this guy named Corey Lewandowski. He used to work for the Koch family. And I'm going to announce in June. I want you to be one of my media surrogates."

It's only in looking back that I see how significant that moment was. If I had had a crystal ball, I would have jumped at the opportunity and might be in a completely different place right now. Then again, if I could see the future of the man behind the desk on the twenty-sixth floor of Trump Tower, I might not be writing this book. As it happened, I still didn't believe he was running for president, and even if I did, I couldn't have joined his campaign. I already had my candidate.

The strength of my strong fund-raising for Mitt, and the fact that SALT's reputation was gaining each year, put me in a pretty good position to sign on with whatever campaign I wanted in the 2016 cycle. Though conventional establishment wisdom would have told me to throw in with Jeb Bush, I didn't want to be a small fry in a prime-rib dinner. Jeb, the presumptive frontrunner, had a huge war chest and an army of people working for him. Had I joined his campaign right away, I would have been riding on the seventieth campaign bus, not riding right next to the candidate. No one would have known my name. So instead of signing on with Jeb, I found someone whose campaign was a bit more modest.

I first met Wisconsin governor Scott Walker at a Republican Governors Association event in Aspen. Walker was a reformer, working to make his state more efficient. He'd built a war chest in the Wisconsin treasury, like a rainy-day fund. Not your typical politician, he was a decent, regular guy, and he rode a motorcycle. I told him about Ghost Motorcycle and showed him a picture of my eighty-seven-year-old uncle riding a Harley with my seventy-eight-year-old mom in the sidecar. We hit it off right away.

At the time, Walker's campaign had started making some noise. He had given a speech in January 2015 at the Iowa Freedom Summit that had catapulted him to the top of the Republican presidential field. His performance at the historic theater Hoyt Sherman Place brought the packed crowd to its feet. It even overwhelmed the appearance of Donald Trump. (Mr. Trump did leave his mark on the event, though. The *Des Moines Register* called him "the most brazen speaker to take the stage.")

None of that seemed to matter to Mr. Trump, who sat waiting for my answer.

"It's already too late," I said. I told him about Walker.

Mr. Trump didn't blink.

"What if I kill Walker?" he said.

"Well, then I have a relationship with Woody Johnson," I said with a shrug. The Johnson and Johnson heir and owner of the New York Jets, who'd been a good friend of mine for years, was then siding with Jeb Bush. I'd made promises to him.

"I'd have to go with Jeb," I said.

Mr. Trump didn't look disappointed at all. His expression, that "negotiating face" you've seen him wear on television and in photos, didn't change one iota. In looking back, I now believe he might have been disappointed if I had accepted right away. There would be no sport in it that way, and Donald Trump loves to fight for what he wants. Plus, as the entire Washington establishment learned the hard way during the 2016 campaign, nothing fuels him more than people counting him out.

Trump looked me straight in the eyes.

"All right," he said. "After I kill Walker and I kill Jeb, you're gonna come work for me?"

I shook his hand and told him we had a deal. As I stepped out of Trump Tower onto Fifth Avenue that morning, I thought my chances of working for Donald Trump were about as good as my chances of playing shortstop for the New York Yankees. Not for one second did I think he would outlast Scott Walker, never mind Jeb Bush, who had more money and Washington influence behind him than almost any candidate who'd ever run for the top office. Hell, I still wasn't convinced he was actually going to leave *The Apprentice*.

Y ET FOUR MONTHS later, there he was descending a golden escalator in the atrium of Trump Tower with his beautiful wife, Melania, about to announce the Donald J. Trump for President campaign. I'm sure you've seen clips of that moment over the years. It looked, on television at least, like the atrium was packed with adoring fans. I would learn later from a few friends on the campaign that all of that was smoke and mirrors. There wasn't a big crowd at all. They had given building workers Make America Great Again T-shirts and had them line the balcony so the place would look full. That was the first and last time the campaign would have to stack the deck. Though Manhattan is Donald Trump's home, a legion of supporters, his base, waited on the road.

Mr. Trump had invited me to the announcement, but I was tied up with something at my office. By 2015, my participation in politics had become a lot more refined than it was during my early days of haphazard political donations to friends of my clients. I'd hired a woman named Amanda Ober to be political director. Amanda kept me abreast of the political landscape and helped me navigate the maze of political contributions. That morning, I sent Amanda to Trump Tower.

I watched the announcement on the TV in my office. Like many, I first thought the illegal immigration portion of the speech was narrow minded. The working-class Americans who live under the constant threat of job competition and the heroin that comes daily over the border from Mexico never entered my mind. While my brother was helping out a kid on Long Island who'd gotten hooked on cheap heroin, most likely from over the border, I was up in my fancy office shaking my head because Donald Trump had said some rude things. Looking back, I still think his words were too rough. Part of the president's immigration policy is a leftover from Bannon's reign as presidential advisor and strategist. Some strategist. His policy would go on to produce photos of hysterical small children after being separated from their parents at the border. Bannon "the brain," my ass.

Though Mr. Trump's announcement garnered a great deal of attention (most of it negative), it certainly didn't convince me that Walker, or any other Republican candidate, had anything to worry about.

GOVERNOR WALKER OFFICIALLY announced his candidacy on July 15, 2015 (I had been unofficially on his team since that previous January), and three days later I thought the Donald J. Trump campaign was dust.

It was then, at a forum in Iowa, when Mr. Trump told an interviewer that he didn't think John McCain was a war hero. I remember thinking either he was trying to purposely crater his campaign or he was doing something that I didn't completely understand.

It was the latter.

Before I try to unpack Trump's statement, first let me make a couple of things clear. John McCain is a bona fide American hero. I have the utmost respect for the sacrifices that members of our military make during the time of war. My uncle Anthony, for whom I was named, was in a Higgins boat that landed on the beach at Normandy. He was lucky that he wasn't in the first row of that boat—those soldiers were shot and killed as the ramp opened in the shallow water. On the beach more of his boatmates were killed. He was spared only because he saw a soldier he was friendly with run right though a stretch of the beach that was lined with mines and barbed wire. My uncle followed him, and he too survived. They realized that the minefield must have been a decoy. They were right. The Germans had run out of live mines and put the casings in the sand. My uncle and his friend radioed back to their captain, and most of their unit was able to get safely to the base of the cliffs under the German pillboxes. Uncle Anthony was awarded the Purple Heart and the French Croix de Guerre, among many other medals. The horror and death he saw on that beach and in other campaigns during the war were nearly too much for him. He certainly suffered some level of PTSD. He said nothing about his experience in the war, not a word, to anyone until 1998. That was the year that *Saving Private Ryan* was released. Watching that powerful film opened a door in him that had been locked for fifty-four years.

So yes, I have enormous respect for members of our military. If you have even a scintilla of doubt of the horror McCain had to endure, I urge you to Google "The Weasel, Twelve Monkeys and the Shrub," a profile of the senator by David Foster Wallace that ran in *Rolling Stone* magazine in 2000. Read the opening paragraphs of that piece, and then tell me you don't have an enormous amount of gratitude and empathy for the senator's sacrifice. As I write this, Senator McCain is gravely ill with brain cancer, and my only hope for him is that his journey ahead is filled with those who love him.

It should be noted, however, that Senator McCain was not sick with brain cancer when Mr. Trump made the remark. Furthermore, McCain had been a staunch detractor of the Trump campaign from the moment of Mr. Trump's announcement. Though Senator McCain had once been considered a maverick of the Senate, he had long since settled into the Republican establishment and ruling class of DC. There is no bigger threat to DC's ruling class than Donald Trump, and Senator McCain knew this better than anyone.

For Donald Trump, on the other hand, politics is a game. He never saw it as anything other than that. He approached his campaign secure in the knowledge that he had a real job waiting for him at home. If his campaign had cratered, he would have shrugged and headed right back to Trump Tower. There's a story my friends David Bossie and Corey Lewandowski, both of whom worked on the Trump campaign (and wrote a book about it: *Let Trump Be Trump*), tell about Mr. Trump on election night. Early in the evening, he was in his residence on top of Trump Tower with Melania. His son-in-law, Jared, called to tell him that the early returns didn't look good for him. He snapped his flip phone closed and tossed it on the bed.

"Jared says we're going to lose," he told his wife. "What a waste of time and money."

For Mr. Trump, the object of the game was to vanquish the other players. To do so, he used whatever was at his disposal. He saw John McCain as a status-quo politician and a formidable block to his objective. His only purpose in making the remark was to move that block out of his way.

Because it was a game, he also liked to have fun playing it. Though it might be hard for some to understand, many of his most controversial statements actually come from his sense of humor. I often call Mr. Trump the first shock-jock candidate. Not unlike Howard

Stern, on whose show he was a guest many times, Mr. Trump's humor at times depends on shocking people. In his wonderful book *Win Bigly*, Scott Adams contends that Mr. Trump's humor is a product of him being a New Yorker. "An average New Yorker," he writes, "thinks the inappropriateness of the joke is what makes it funny."

Though Mr. Trump might be having fun, anyone who doesn't think there is also a political calculation attached to what he says is sorely mistaken. What few realized at the time is that his attack on Senator McCain sent red meat to his base. It gave them notice that he was going to come in and disrupt the way things stood, and he was going to do it in the only way he knew how: by saying something you couldn't miss. He had also talked about caring for vets in every one of his rallies, and he knew he had them on his side.

His first public appearance after the McCain remark, just three days later, was in Sun City, South Carolina. The rally at a retirement community favored by military families was filled with vets. He received three standing ovations during his speech, and there wasn't a single sign in protest. That event was also remarkable for another reason. Continuing his shock campaign against status-quo politicians, he gave out Lindsey Graham's cell phone number to the crowd. Even though I was deep in Walker's camp, when I heard about it I laughed out loud. To his credit, Graham would see the humor in it too and turn the episode into a favorable one, something John McCain never did. Before you jump all over me, I'm aware that the gravity of the two events isn't even close. You have to wonder, however, how the relationship between McCain and the president, and the charged political atmosphere that surrounded it, could have been different had the senator reacted more like Graham.

Mr. Trump's impulses, while they often get him into trouble, are still a negative side effect of a very savvy campaign strategy—one that got him elected in the first place.

For instance, he thumbs his nose at the media. If he knows they want him to say one thing, he'll say exactly the opposite, or as close to the opposite as he can get. The presser after Charlottesville, for example. He knew that every reporter lined up at his press conference wanted him to give a stock phrase: I condemn white nationalism and neo-Nazis and all that they stand for. Had he said it, he would have felt like he was letting the media, who'd already been very unfair to him, write the narrative for him. His refusal to say what the media and the Left wanted him to didn't mean he was siding with the neo-Nazis. He just wasn't going to let anyone dictate his words.

In all other areas of life but the presidency, people seem to root for the outsider. They want to see the underdog prevail against a system that's keeping everyone down. When a company disrupts a market with a new technology that makes all others obsolete, we all buy stock in that company. The company founder's face gets put on magazine covers and we want him to succeed. When a musician like Chance the Rapper or French Montana comes from outside the traditional record label infrastructure and starts making hits anyway, we all buy the records. We like it when people buck the system and pave their own way.

But when it comes to the presidency we don't seem to have the same open-mindedness. We're too blinded by the pomp and circumstance of the office. The tradition. We believe that there's some solemn, priestly quality that anyone ascending to the Oval must have. Maybe it's a holdover from the darker days of our history, when we chose kings rather than elected representatives because we thought there was something divine about them. With all the ceremonial trimmings that have come to define the office, it's easy to view the presidency in the same exalted way. We've set a standard of excellence and poise that no human being could ever live up to.

The ones who seem to live up to our unrealistic standard are just actors playing a role.

What we often forget is that the presidency, at its root, is a job like any other. It's a tough job, and one that involves effectively managing over 4 million people who work for the federal government and setting policy for the 350 million or so people who live in the United States, but it's got the same day-to-day challenges of running a grocery store or a Fortune 500 company. It requires the same quick thinking and ingenuity as working in the private sector. This is why Donald Trump is fundamentally suited for the office.

I know this now. Back after the McCain remark, however, the only office I thought he was suited for was on the twenty-sixth floor of Trump Tower.

CHAPTER THIRTEEN

THE LOOPHOLE

After the first Republican primary debate in Cleveland, August 6, 2015.
(Scott Olsen / Getty Images News)

I N APRIL OF 1939, only three months before Fred Trump would park the famous Trump Show Boat off the coast of Coney Island and give out $250 coupons to beachgoers, Franklin Delano Roosevelt became the first president in history to have his picture put on TV. He spoke from the grounds of the 1939 World's Fair, the theme of which was "The World of Tomorrow," and the world's first operational television camera caught the whole thing. His speech was televised live on a black-and-white RCA television set, which had been set up on a stage for spectators and dealers of home electronics to view.

As we now know, this was an event that changed the course of American history. Before that day, the president of the United States existed to citizens as either a voice on the radio or words printed in a newspaper—sometimes, for people who could afford it, he was a speck on a faraway stage or a few seconds of newsreel footage shown in a movie theater. But as soon as FDR initiated the World's Fair in Queens, and the people watching on a box got a better view than the people right in front of him, a new era in American politics was inaugurated.

The era of the television would follow, a time when camera crews cropped up all around the country and there was a television set in every living room; when families gathered by the millions to watch the president speak directly from his office in the White House. It was an era in which we pitted candidates who could be charming on television, like Dwight Eisenhower (after a *Mad Men* makeover), John F. Kennedy, and Ronald Reagan, against candidates such as Adlai Stevenson, Richard Nixon, and Jimmy Carter, who were… less than charming. In the era of the television, it became abundantly clear which candidates had charisma, and which ones didn't.

Today, with the internet becoming more dominant than ever, that era is quickly nearing its end. I would be willing to bet that Donald J. Trump was the last (given the dominance of the internet), and by far the greatest, of the television candidates. His rise to the presidency was the climax to a broadcast that began in 1939, and anything after it will quickly disappear like credits rolling on a screen.

Although I, along with most of the political world, still doubted his chances, Mr. Trump's performance at the first Republican primary debate in August 2015 proved that he was a candidate like none who had come before. You remember the night, right? It was the debate where Megyn Kelly came out with what she was sure was a knockout punch. "You've called women fat pigs, slobs, dogs," she began. It wasn't a fair question. It was mean spirited and used comments taken out of context and distilled from a lifetime of interviews and appearances from a man who led the world in interviews and appearances. Had she asked any other candidate the same question it would have been devastating, a campaign ender. She didn't, though. She asked Donald Trump, and Donald Trump might be best counterpuncher in political history. My hunch was Roger Ailes who didn't like Trump encouraged the question.

"Only Rosie O'Donnell," he said in response.

As the hall exploded in laughter, Megyn Kelly looked steadfast and a little shocked, while he beamed with an expression that said, "You want to mix it up with the Trumpster, you better be down with the consequences."

The Loophole

When the laughter finally settled, Mr. Trump went on to say that the insistence on political correctness in this country is one of our biggest problems. The applause was deafening.

I know. I was in the audience that night, and what I saw was a master class in television communication. I saw a man so confident in his element, so above the others onstage, it was like watching Joe DiMaggio play for Schreiber High School's baseball team. Without question, Donald Trump's social media following and skills helped him win the election. He became the Republican nominee, however, because of the way he delivered his candidacy and platform in the debates on TV.

From my seat in the audience, I began to wonder how long Scott Walker could withstand the onslaught. Hell, I began to wonder how long anyone could.

In my few years of being on television—which, admittedly, is not even close to Donald Trump's, but it's a little more than most people get—I've learned a few things about the camera, chief among them that it knows when you're being inauthentic. The lens is a lot like your mother in that way. Your mother knows when you're lying; at least, my mother did.

Whatever you might think about him, Donald J. Trump was the only authentic candidate on television in 2015. He might have been the only truly authentic candidate in history. He knew better than most that if you try to tamp down your demons on television, they'll only come out screaming when it's least convenient for you. So he played to his strengths, and he won. He made jokes, gave nicknames, and sucked up every bit of air on those stages until the rest of the candidates could hardly breathe. Most serious theater actors would be envious of how well he commanded the audiences.

Part of this was innate talent. Another part was worldliness. But the most important part, to which people don't give nearly enough consideration, is practice. By the time the debates rolled around, Donald Trump had put more hours into developing his voice and persona for television than any candidate in American electoral history—second only to Ronald Reagan, perhaps, who'd spent his whole life in front of the cameras in Hollywood. The difference is that Reagan mostly read other people's words from scripts, whereas whenever Donald Trump went on television, he had to be himself, which he did perfectly. Even on the shows he made brief appearances on—which, though many connected with those shows might not like to brag about it now, include everything from *Fresh Prince of Bel-Air* and *Sex and the City* to *Top Gear* and *Inside the Actors Studio*—he was never anything other than the same character, sharpening his skills like a pitcher in the bullpen. He also knew how good he was. Oliver Stone cast him to play himself in *Wall Street: Money Never Sleeps*, the movie in which I had a small role. Mr. Trump's character didn't make the cut, but his performance still impressed the director. "It's very easy to get charmed by Donald Trump," Oliver said.

"Charmed" might not be the word the other Republican primary candidates would have used to describe Donald Trump on TV. It got to the point where you wondered why anyone would get into a one-on-one with him—he knows how to fight in a cage.

One afternoon, however, I found myself exactly in that position. This was in August of 2015, and I was still fretting over the candidacy of Scott Walker, for whom I was still raising money and being a surrogate for despite his shaky performance at the first debate. I had made the rounds on television and, in so many words, said that maybe Donald Trump was not as serious a candidate as people were making him out to be and that he should probably step aside for true conservatives like Jeb Bush and my pal Scott Walker. I hadn't thought much about my actual choice of words at the time, which might have been a bit sarcastic, and I definitely didn't think Mr. Trump was watching.

That was a mistake. As many political pundits and news-show hosts would later find out, you talk trash about Donald Trump on television at your own peril. He sees everything.

Before I could even recall my solemn vow not to piss him off, he was halfway through a tirade about me—well, my industry—telling a packed stadium in the middle of the country that I and other "hedge fund guys" were the enemy. I never thought I'd feel bad for the press, but jeez, I can't imagine what it'd be like to be on the receiving end of that every day. I kept watching, and it only got worse.

"The hedge fund guys," he said. "They didn't build this country. These are guys that shift paper around and they get lucky...They make a fortune. They pay no tax. It's ridiculous. Some of them are friends of mine; some of them I could care less about. It is the wrong thing. They're getting away with murder."

I should say, in the interest of calling balls and strikes, that the guy wasn't totally wrong. Most people outside Wall Street would probably agree with him, and for valid reasons. In fact, with those few words, Donald Trump entered one of the most fraught debates in modern fiscal policy. The debate involves an obscure piece of financial law known as the carried-interest loophole, which, according to its critics, is little more than a crooked tax dodge—although SkyBridge doesn't benefit from it—that allows investors like Mitt Romney and me to get out of paying our fair share of income tax. Not exactly accurate, and I'll tell you why.

Allow me to get a little wonky (or skip the next few pages).

In the United States, the amount that each citizen owes in taxes is determined by the Internal Revenue Code. The code contains all the rules and rates for taxes on income, store-bought items, and assets, like stocks, bonds, boats, and houses. It also grants relief from taxes to some people, most of which can be taken in the form of deductions, for things like charitable donations or having children. Deductions are mostly for things the government wants to encourage. How much you end up paying, however, often depends on how much you make.

There were seven income-tax brackets. Depending on which one you fall into, you usually pay between 10 and 40 percent in taxes. Taxes on assets, however—meaning things you buy and keep for a while, like stocks, bonds, boats, and houses—fall into two camps. They're either taxed as "long-term capital gains," which means you pay at a rate of around 15 percent, or "short-term capital gains," which are taxed just like regular income. I should note that these tax rates don't matter until you sell the asset; they technically kick in when you sign over the boat or the house and someone gives you money in return. That money is the thing that gets taxed, not the asset itself.

Under the current rules, if you held the boat or the house for longer than twelve months, you would pay the long-term capital gains rate on the money you get when you sell it, which means you keep much more of the money for yourself. If you held that asset for less than a year, on the other hand, you would pay taxes on that money just like it was regular income from your job—which, if you're talking about houses and boats, probably means you're forking over 30 percent or so of your boat money to Uncle Sam. When you're dealing with hundreds of thousands of dollars, this makes a huge difference. Which it's supposed to. Having such a low tax on long-term capital gains encourages people to hold on to their investments, which helps the American economy grow and prosper. It also serves as the basic principle underlying many retirement and investment accounts in the United States, allowing people to put money away that would normally be taxed at a high rate, then withdraw it years down the line at a reduced rate.

Still with me? Okay, but I'm sure you're thinking, what in the world does this have to do with hedge funds? Well, you've hung with me this far, so I'll tell you.

It has to do with the way hedge fund managers make money. Because they don't have a boss who cuts a check every week, they need to derive their income directly from clients, which is usually done through a simple arrangement, standard among the partners of hedge funds. Under this arrangement, when you invest your money in a hedge fund, you agree to pay a 2 percent management fee, which barely covers operating costs. However, you, being the benevolent titan of industry that you are, also agree to pay 20 percent of all the money we make together.

For example: You give the manager $100, which he and his team invest for you. That $100 then turns into, say, $1,002. (It's my book; I can dream.) You're ecstatic. You high-five. You then pay $2 as the management fee, then 20 percent of the $900 you and the hedge fund manager made together. In total, you walk away with about $700 for doing pretty much nothing, and the hedge fund manager— the person who designed the investment strategies—gets a little under $200 for their trouble. That part might give some people pause, but it's not controversial. Those are terms that were agreed to.

Here's where it gets hairy.

That money is all "income," at least in spirit. The checks go straight to the hedge fund, where it goes toward paying employees, renting the office space, and getting new K-Cups for the office. But according to the letter of the tax code, that money you gave the hedge fund manager actually did not go to the manager personally. It was, for all intents and purposes, invested in the hedge fund, with no stipulation as to when the manager has to pull it out and treat it as personal income. It could be left in the fund forever if that was what the manager wanted and allowed to continue to create value for the fund as the market dipped and shifted. The manager could also pull it out immediately and pay the short-term capital-gains rate on it, which would effectively make it income, just like the money I used to make at Espresso Pizza at Tufts or from my *Long Island Newsday* paper route. But hedge funds don't.

Instead, they hold it in the fund for twelve months, wait, and take it out when it can be taxed at 15 percent, as a long-term capital gain. It saves the manager an enormous amount in taxes, and lets them make even bigger plays next time. To some people, this means they're "dodging" taxes and screwing over people who have to pay a full, nonnegotiable percentage of their income—the old Warren Buffett line that his secretary pays a higher tax rate than he does. I get that. But to others, it just means the manager is taking advantage of the rules as they exist, and to do otherwise would be to deny free money, which is bad business. The truth, as usual, is somewhere in between. That is, most of these managers are in the top bracket for income tax, which means that for every dollar they make, something like sixty cents goes either to the federal government or the governments of the state and towns they live in. So, a hedge fund manager that makes $1 million will pay $600,000 in taxes. (I pay between $4 and $5 million in taxes each year. Don't get me wrong; I don't mind. But I think that's about equal to my fair share.)

The break they get with carried interest is also a reward for working in a high-risk environment. Hedge fund managers don't make any money unless they make the right plays in the market. And if they make the wrong plays, they, and their employees, are liable to lose everything they have. It's an uncomfortable position to be in, and the extra cushion they get from the carried-interest cash helps ensure they won't go under because of a few bad trades or a market meltdown.

Now, you might be asking, is that really fair? Maybe it's not. But it's the way the system has been set up, and hedge fund managers are not in the business of turning down free money. Just like Donald Trump—who, believe me, knows his loopholes better than a midshipman in the Navy. Remember his "That makes me smart" response to the tax question during the debate with Hillary? A savvy hedge fund manager should take advantage of the system as it is. This, coupled with the fact that tax revenue from carried interest makes up a tiny fraction of what the IRS takes in every year, lets them sleep with a clear conscience, as it should.

Of course, the above long-winded explanation of the tax loophole mattered little to the people to whom Donald Trump was speaking. All they heard was that hedge fund guys were "getting away with murder." Part of his genius as a candidate is to boil down the most complex issue to bite-size language. In doing so, he brought the debate down to a level where he is masterful. Many people much smarter than I have fallen into his trap and tried to wrestle him in the mud. No one beats him in the mud.

And yet that's where I found myself. Getting dirty with Donald Trump. I went back on Fox Business, and leveled some choice words at him. (I also, for the record, called him "Donald," so you know I was getting into it with him.) I said he was a "political hack," an "inherited-money dude from Queens County," and that he would be president of the Queens County Bully Association. I may or may not have challenged him to a fight as well; I'm not really sure.

Yikes, right?

On *Fox and Friends* he came right back at me.

For a while, I was looking over my shoulder, but then he called and said he wanted to see me.

"Why are you hitting me so hard?" he asked me in his office on top of Trump Tower.

"You started it!" I said. "Besides, you're the guy who told me I should counterpunch!"

He laughed, it was all part of the game, and again asked if I wanted to join his campaign.

I told him I couldn't, that I'd given my word to the governor, and he commended me on my loyalty.

As it turned out, the ship I was loyal to was about to sink.

J UST ONE MONTH after the Megyn Kelly debate, in September 2015, with dismal poll numbers and an unfriendly financial outlook, Walker's campaign was staggering. Not that it mattered. Mr. Trump's lead was by then already nearly insurmountable. Governor Walker had one last shot—the Republican primary debate at the Ronald Reagan Library in mid-September 2015. With Reagan's Air Force One as the backdrop, the debate opened as a full-out assault against Mr. Trump. Governor Walker was game, and offered up a few good lines. "We don't need an apprentice in the White House…We have one right now," he said. But to quote the great political mind Yogi Berra, it was getting late early for the Wisconsin governor.

That week after the Reagan debate I took a much-needed family vacation down to Disney World, where I take the kids every year. While there, Scott Walker called me.

He was in a good mood for someone who was getting his teeth kicked in. He was gracious and grateful for my help, but, he said, he was getting out of the race before, as he put it, "Trump gives me a nickname."

Walker fulfilled his campaign pledge to back the Republican nominee. He spoke at the Republican convention on behalf of Mr. Trump and campaigned actively for the candidate in Wisconsin— he was one of the principal reasons Mr. Trump carried the state. (The Trump team returned the favor. About a week after Election

Day, Vice President-Elect Mike Pence and I organized a fund-raiser at my restaurant to help Walker retire his campaign debt.)

I'd put in six weeks as Walker's finance cochair. We had hosted fund-raisers in Chicago, New York, Florida, and out in the Hamptons. I spent time in his office in Madison, Wisconsin, and he came to New York to use my office for debate prep. I, like many others, thought Scott Walker could make an impact during the primary cycle. He was a scrapper with midwestern appeal. As governor of Wisconsin, he battled through a recall election. He faced down one hundred thousand prounion protestors. He ultimately stripped the public-sector unions of their right to collective bargaining and to collect dues from their members. I am a prounion person; always have been. But in every union people have to have some personal accountability. The way those union contracts were structured, people who weren't doing the job were getting paid as much as those who were. It's like what happens in New York City. The teachers' union there has something called "the Rubber Room," which has nothing to do with mental well-being. The Rubber Room is where they put bad teachers that they can't bounce out of a job. What Walker did was rightsize those unions. I guess in one way, though, backing Walker completed my separation from the Long Island politics of my youth, of my father, of Joltin' Joe Margiotta. I was on a path that was taking me deep into the land of establishment Republicans.

As I HAD promised Woody Johnson, and told Donald Trump, I got right to work fund-raising for Jeb. I thought he would've been a strong business-minded president. He knew Wall Street, and had worked for Lehman Brothers after his two terms as Florida's governor. He was with the ill-fated bank right until the end and tried desperately to raise the capital to keep it afloat. Two weeks before Lehman collapsed, Jeb was in Mexico City trying to coax billionaire Carlos Slim to help. Mr. Slim wouldn't, and Lehman fell, but Jeb stayed on with Barclays Bank, which took over what was left of Lehman.

Though I thought he'd make a good president, I wasn't all that convinced Jeb would get the chance. Soon after I joined his campaign, I attended a luncheon at the Hunt & Fish Club (the event was hosted by Robert Wolf, my partner in the restaurant) where the pollster Frank Luntz spoke. Luntz was there to discuss Mr. Trump's campaign and whether there were any places he might be vulnerable. I told the crowd that one of Mr. Trump's greatest assets as a candidate is that people underestimate him. Governor Walker underestimated him. Jeb already had. The whole Republican Party did. I said that if he got the nomination, Hillary Clinton would underestimate him too.

"You don't want Donald Trump sneaking up on you," I said.

Around the time I was giving that speech, Donald Trump was sneaking up on us—just not in the way anyone expected. He had been releasing policy proposals for a few months at that point, most of which contained the kind of undoable, wild points you'd expect from his campaign. When I found out he was coming out with a tax plan, I expected some crazy stuff. But, as it turned out, his plan wasn't crazy at all. He wanted to cut the number of income tax brackets from seven to four, and lower taxes substantially for everyone. It's the same plan Republicans had been touting since Reagan, and there was hardly anything different about it. There was, of course, a Trumpian flourish in the thing, which I enjoyed. In the section of the plan that said Trump would eliminate income tax altogether for people making under $25,000 a year, the plan said that those people would get a one-page tax form to send to the IRS. The page could be filled out with just two words: "I win."

The Loophole

As I kept reading, I found that he had totally dropped his objections to the carried-interest deduction altogether—which, if you'll remember, was the one thing that I had been ready to go to war with him over!

In the months that followed, he said he'd realized that eliminating the loophole would only save the government about $1 billion a year, but that the larger tax cuts could do one hundred times that amount. And just like that, under the radar, he'd dropped it from his plan. This is a model that Donald Trump continues to follow to this day. He makes a lot of noise about something, starts up a conversation about it, pitting people against each other to generate a healthy amount of argument and chaos, then works behind the scenes while no one's looking to get things done. It's part of the living library strategy I've mentioned in describing my father. For all I know, Trump was floating the idea of eliminating the deduction, waiting to see what I and a few dozen other people were going to say. Then, when we said it and argued with each other, he made his decision. I've watched him do it a hundred times since then, and it always takes me by surprise.

Looking back, it was then that it began to dawn on me. Donald J. Trump wasn't the extreme, unhinged, unserious candidate that I thought he was. He knew exactly how the system operated, and he knew how to work it to the advantage of the American people. He knew that the classic Republican tax plan would be good for the country, but he also knew that it was boring as sin, and that a robotic establishment candidate couldn't sell it. Scott Walker and Jeb Bush were great, but not great enough to get anyone excited about taxes.

Guys like them had been failing to do that since 2000, when George W. Bush unveiled something similar and saw his success go down the drain in an unrelated financial crisis. Only someone with courage and a TV star's flare for the dramatic could get people thinking about how unfair the current tax system was. Then, once he'd gotten the public's attention with something that benefited them directly, he started mentioning our trade deals—how they were unfair, lopsided, and in desperate need of reform. Even if other candidates happened to agree with him, they never would have been able to get anyone listening to why. Jeb would have been up onstage at one of his rallies with a laser pointer and PowerPoint slides on economic singularities and trade deficits, all while people fell asleep in the stands. Donald Trump, on the other hand, knew exactly how much of the issue people could take, and why the issue mattered in simplified terms. He did it by cutting through the loaded, overly complex language politicians have been spouting for years. Another candidate might drone on and on (as I did above) about an issue such as trade with China, whereas Mr. Trump would throw up his hands and say, "Everything is made in China!" and the crowd would be ready to grab torches and pitchforks.

THANKS TO DONALD Trump—despite what you might have heard on the news—2016 was the first presidential campaign in recent memory when people were actually talking about issues rather than banal phrases dressed up as issues. Sure, they spent a lot of time on the celebrity aspect of it all, but along the way they picked up more hard knowledge about immigration reform, the tax code, and the way Washington works than at any time before. I can't think of another time in history when people on the street would know not only the names of the vice-presidential nominees for both parties but the full policy positions and campaign managers too. Whether the coverage was all positive or not, it got people involved.

I've often said that we should follow the lead of countries like Australia and institute mandatory voting. That way, politicians will have to talk to everyone and not just their bases. While I don't think that's politically feasible, I think a candidate like Donald Trump, who injected a little life and levity into the political process, was the next best thing.

Unfortunately, not everyone got the message. And most of the candidates who did got it too late. As for Jeb, well, he just wasn't the right candidate to do battle with Mr. Trump, especially in front of the cameras. By February, the press was already writing Jeb's obituary. On February 3, the *Los Angeles Times* ran a headline that read, "Where Jeb Went Horribly Wrong." On the same day, a headline in *Vanity Fair* read, "A Condensed Timeline of Jeb Bush's Psychological Breakdown." On February 9, *GQ* called a story they ran about him "The 15 Saddest Moments of His Presidential Campaign." Then on February 20, 2016, Jeb made it official. Two hours after the polls closed for the South Carolina primary, he announced he was dropping out of the race. Mr. Trump had killed him, just like he said he would.

In the gloomy aftermath of Jeb's announcement my phone rang. The voice on the line was familiar.

"When are you coming to my office?" Mr. Trump asked.

CHAPTER FOURTEEN

ALBUQUERQUE

Trump Force One! (Scaramucci family collection)

The crowd at the Albuquerque Trump rally. (Chip Somodevilla / Getty Images)

I N 1980, George H. W. Bush was engaged in a surprisingly bitter primary battle with Ronald Reagan. One of the ways Bush got under Reagan's skin during the primary battle was to use the phrase "voodoo economics" to describe Reagan's approach to trade and taxes. Bush wanted to convince people that the fiscal policy of the Reagan administration was half baked and based on faulty math; it was the only recourse he had against Reagan's movie-star charm and attractive tax proposals. Use of the phrase, as it turned out, worked pretty well. Bush managed to drum up enough dislike for Reagan and his advisors to get pretty close to the nomination but, as you know, not close enough.

Once he'd secured the nomination, however, Reagan named George H. W. Bush as his running mate, which is the surprising part. In the beginning of their working relationship, Bush would stubbornly hold on to opinions about Reagan's economic policy, which caused some contention. Eventually, Bush would come around, and the two men worked well together through eight years in the White House. Still, the phrase "voodoo economics" would end up costing George H. W. Bush a whole lot of political capital, mostly because of how the economy responded to Reaganomics. In the decade after Reagan took office, and American businesses added 20 million new jobs.

Years later, according to Bush's biographer Jon Meacham, when Bush's criticisms of Reagan's economic policy were getting him in trouble with the Republican Party, he would joke to his speechwriter Pete Teeley, who'd come up with the phrase during the primaries, that it was "the only goddamned memorable thing" he'd ever written for him.

I tell you that story because I thought of George H. W. and his phrase, and might even have used it, when I apologized to Mr. Trump for my remarks on television. Though I did apologize, I never caved on principle. I told him my marginal tax rate was over 50 percent, that I paid $4 to $5 million dollars a year in taxes, and that I thought what I paid was more than enough. It was the old #SorryNotSorry trick, as the millennials (a generation of which I'm now an honorary member, according to the fellas at *Barstool Sports*) might call it.

Though my tussle with Mr. Trump played loudly in my head, it wasn't even a whisper in his ear. When I apologized, he shrugged. "I hit you; you hit me back," he said. In the mind of Donald Trump, standing up for yourself earns you respect, not scorn. The only thing he'll end a relationship over is whining or obsequiousness or outright disloyalty. A scrum with Mr. Trump was never a problem. He wanted my help, and wanted to get to work.

"By the way," he said as we shook hands. "Let me give you the name of a good accountant."

★ ∕ ★ ∕ ★

MR. TRUMP WANTED me aboard his train primarily to help him with fund-raising. He'd been running a garage-band campaign since early 2015, with most of the money to fund it coming straight from his bank account and small donors from his Facebook page, and now it was time to add a more traditional approach.

Albuquerque

Keeping the campaign running and getting it ready to beat Hillary Clinton would mean lots of dinners, handshakes, phone calls, and a narrative for the candidate to accentuate the parts of his policy that would suit his audience. I decided a small team and I could make that happen, and I began drawing up hubs of support around the country. When I left his office in Trump Tower, the Trump Train had again left the station. This time, I was on it.

It didn't take long, however, for me to realize how bumpy the ride could be.

Going from Jeb Bush's campaign to Mr. Trump's was like going from backup singer for the Cowsills to playing drums for Ozzy Osbourne. Just in the two weeks surrounding Jeb dropping out of the race, Donald Trump called Ted Cruz a "pussy" (actually, he repeated what a woman in the crowd had said), David Duke tweeted that he loved him, and he got in a fight with the pope. Any one of those events would have crushed the life out of the campaign of another candidate. For Mr. Trump, they weren't even bumps in the road.

Not only did he sidestep any consequences, but he also turned them to his advantage. Especially when it came to his interaction with the pope.

Now, I'm a Catholic, though of the lapsed variety, and even though I don't go to mass much anymore, I hold my Catholic values close and try to live my life by them as much as possible. Thank God (literally) that we Catholics have something called confession. The Handi Wipe of sacraments, confession allows us a clean slate even, for instance, after using the most vulgar language. Given that, you might think I would have sided with Francis against Donald Trump. I didn't. Like many Catholics, Protestants, and those of many religions from around the world, I found the pope's remarks disappointing.

In so many words, Francis had said that Mr. Trump was not a Christian for trying to build a Mexican border wall. It seemed out of character for a pope to judge what is the most personal of matters— one's faith. And that doesn't even broach the subject of the hypocrisy of the remarks. You don't think the pontiff was hypocritical? Well, buy a plane ticket to Rome, then take a cab to the gates of Vatican City, and grab one of those big brass knockers. When the holy pontiff (or his valet) opens the door, ask him if he would mind if you stayed for . . . like the rest of your life. See what he says. I know, I know. The analogy is faulty. The detrimental result of illegal immigration, however, is pretty solid. As the great economist Milton Friedman once put it, you can't have a welfare state without secure borders. In other words, you can't help those less fortunate unless you curb immigration. Otherwise, you'll have people from all over the world rushing in to take advantage of the resources you're offering, and you'll actually lose the ability to care for the citizens you set out to protect in the first place. People make the issue of immigration seem hopelessly complicated, and on a human level it certainly can be; but at root, it really isn't.

We have a well-established process of gaining citizenship to the United States, and it's one of the things that should make us proudest about living here. My grandparents used it. So did Donald Trump's grandparents. I'd be surprised if your relatives didn't use it as well. That poem by Emma Lazarus that adorns the base of the Statue of Liberty is wonderful—every word of it. The United States of America should be a beacon for the tired and hungry of the world, anyone "yearning to breathe free." But freedom, as the bumper stickers say, isn't actually free. We have to pay for it every day in labor and tax dollars. Part of living here is either becoming part of that system, or letting the government know you need some help until you can be. If we continue to let people slip in, undocumented and unaccounted for, the country will see an enormous strain on its resources, especially at the local level, where it matters most. As I said, I was as shocked as anyone with the way Mr. Trump talked about the immigration problem in his announcement. But to think that a criminal element wouldn't take advantage of a porous border is naïve. Look at it this way: if you leave a wallet filled with cash on the seat of a New York City subway, there's a chance you'll get it back. There's also the real possibility, however, that you'll never see it again.

The pope, in his infinite wisdom, knows this intimately. As the head of Vatican City, he enjoys the full, unquestioned power of a nation-state. It's beautiful and holds more wealth than most countries in the world. The Catholic Church is also the second-biggest landowner in the world, behind only the United States government. Would you care to venture a guess as to how many uninvited people get to live in Vatican City every year? That would be zero.

Though many were outraged at the pope's remarks, Mr. Trump loved it. In the world of Trump, getting the pope to say something hurtful toward him was far, far better than having him say something nice. The discourse set Twitter on fire. Countless faith writers and columnist wrote rebukes. Even Jeb denounced the pope's words. Then came Mr. Trump's response.

What Francis found out is what many had already known: Donald Trump is not to be trifled with. Dan Scavino, Mr. Trump's social media director, followed the pontiff's remark with a wordless tweet that contained just one photo: the wall around Vatican City.

What's that line about throwing the first stone?

★ ∫ ★ ∫ ★

ALONG WITH FUND-RAISING, and being an on-air surrogate for Mr. Trump, I was part of his economic policy council and finance committee. These were small groups of people from the campaign who could be trusted to know things about trade, taxes, and the economy in general. It sounds a lot more formal than it was.

Instead, as I've already mentioned, Mr. Trump would have private conversations with each of us and then together as a group. In the space between rallies and media interviews, he'd often pull me aside and ask about tariffs or the stock market—things I would have expertise in or a point of view on. Then we'd talk for five or ten minutes, and he'd move on. I would usually forget the majority of what I told him. But he wouldn't. For days after that, I would walk in on him having the same conversation with campaign staffers from other committees, his friends, even members of the media and his family. They'd be giving him their take on the situation just as I did, only with a different slant or emphasis on a particular angle.

On every issue, Donald Trump wanted as much information as he could get. But he never let anyone know he was gathering information to make policy out of it; that might have tainted what people were saying. People tend to get more political than practical when you tell them they're in the hot seat. So he made it seem like he was chatting, talking economics and trade policy the way you'd talk about the New York Mets. Then he synthesized all the responses into one position, letting in the good bits and keeping out the bad. This is what he'd use at his rallies—those coherent and punchy statements that could resonate with stadiums full of people.

One of the things that bothers me the most is when people claim that President Trump is stupid, even if it's only by euphemism or implication. Donald Trump has the kind of knowledge that is different from what people are used to hearing from a president, and for that he's chastised. I know him well, and I believe he has an intellect that is uniquely suited to the presidency. Where some people have passages from Plato and Xenophon in their heads, or have memorized historical scenes from a Morris or McCullough biography,

President Trump has a fifty-year backlog of faces, interactions, deals, and conversations.

A living library, and they're all first editions.

Whenever he's presented with a problem, he consults people, not books, for help. He'll ask anyone who comes into his orbit what they think about a given issue, then ask someone else. Then he'll ask the first guy what he thinks about what the second guy said. Then he'll ask a third guy what the first two thought and bring the third guy's opinion back to the first two. He lets ideas pour into his head like sand, then shakes them around in there until a few grains stick together and make concrete. It's how he won the election, and it's how he's leading the United States through tax reform and a revamping of its infrastructure. It's how he'll decide what course to take in battle, should it ever come to that.

There's a story I've always liked about John F. Kennedy, which I think illustrates this point quite well. It's told through the eyes of Ted Sorenson in his book on the Kennedy presidency, as well as other accounts, and takes place during the height of the Cuban Missile Crisis. The Soviet Union had just stationed nuclear missiles ninety miles off the coast of Florida, and no one was sure what would happen next. The Joint Chiefs, led in large part by Curtis LeMay, a veteran Air Force general, recommended a full-scale strike and invasion. Under Operation Northwoods, the United States military would bomb the island of Cuba and storm the beaches within hours. The generals who'd recommended it were men Kennedy barely knew, but they were believed to be experts in matters of war. Had Kennedy been a more malleable person—or alone in the room without his brother Robert, the attorney general, to bounce ideas off of—he might have agreed with them and carried out the strike.

The result, we later learned, would have been nuclear holocaust.

Instead, Kennedy consulted his brother Bobby and a few other people he trusted. He pored over all the entries from his own living library he could find, and ignored the cold facts presented to him by the Joint Chiefs. In time, he elected to impose a blockade instead. The Soviets stood down, and the conflict was resolved diplomatically—by people in the same room, speaking to one another face-to-face. Years later, when transcripts of the meetings emerged, Kennedy's mounting frustration with his generals became more apparent. He can be heard making jokes at their expense, challenging their authority every few minutes. Sound like anyone you know?

Later, asked by a guest at the White House what advice he'd give his successor, Kennedy said this: "The first thing I'll tell my successor is to watch the generals, and to avoid feeling that just because they were military men, their opinions on military matters were worth a damn."

DONALD TRUMP CONDUCTED his first political campaign, which might have logged more miles than any campaign in political history, while running his business as he always had. Even when he was taking ten plane trips a week, most of which spanned several time zones and business days, he'd be working. Let me give you an example.

In May of 2016, I was traveling with the campaign to a rally in Albuquerque (the one I mentioned at the beginning of the book) and sitting across the aisle from Mr. Trump. He was sitting at his table on Trump Force One, facing the cockpit of the plane, and we were chatting.

A few minutes before we were set to take off, Keith Schiller, Mr. Trump's longtime bodyguard, brought out three large banker's boxes, all brimming with thick bond paper, stapled packets, and manila folders. Then he set them on the floor next to Mr. Trump. They hit the carpet with a thud. Donald Trump looked at them the way I look at a big plate of pasta around dinnertime; he was ready to dig in. But he moved slowly and deliberately as the plane prepared for takeoff, grabbing piles of paper and giving them brief glances as he talked to the people around him. Soon the papers were spread all around the table as if he'd been sitting there all night reviewing them. There were some contracts that needed signing, email print-outs, clippings from newspapers, a few magazines he liked, policy papers, catalogs. More things than I could have read in a week.

And he had a speech to deliver in a few hours!

By the time we were in the air, he was carrying on a full conversation with me, only lifting his head briefly from the papers on the table. I could tell he was paying attention to them, too, because the conversation would shift abruptly based on what he was reading. We covered everything from reporters I knew at the *New York Times*—which Mr. Trump still considers his hometown paper, no matter what he says about them—business deals he'd worked on, and minute details of his properties. I felt like I was face-to-face with an encyclopedia. We'd been talking about Mar-a-Lago, I think, when he picked up a big stack of white pages and began flipping through them. Finally, I got curious.

"What in the world are you doing?" I asked him.

He looked up, one of his fingers still flipping through the stack, and said, "Elevator-equipment contracts. For these new condominiums."

I was a little rattled. "Sir, I thought we were running for president! You've got a speech in like three hours!"

He didn't seem troubled. I was like a fly buzzing by. By the time I'd finished speaking, he was looking down at the elevator contracts again, reaching with his other hand into the inside pocket of his suit jacket, which he'd slung over the back of his chair on the way in. "Relax," he said, holding a folded-up piece of paper in his hand. "Here it is."

He showed me the paper, a.k.a. the New Mexico speech, and I saw nothing but three bullet points in his handwriting—not long ones, either. Just a few notes on what was important to hit, and why it would matter to this particular audience. The rest, he said, would be done extemporaneously. For the remainder of the flight, we continued chatting, and he managed to get through the whole pile of elevator-equipment contracts. In the back of my mind, I did wonder whether he would get serious and write out a whole speech. I thought maybe it was a joke, that we had a teleprompter guy meeting us in Albuquerque. Nope.

Just before we touched down on the tarmac, Mr. Trump stood up and slung his jacket back over his shoulders, having tucked the folded-up speech back into his inside pocket. That was all he needed. He looked at me, one of his eyebrows raised, a smile on his lips. "Do you think Hillary's doing this?" he said. "Running a business from her campaign plane?"

I laughed and said she probably wasn't. I don't think he heard me, though. By then he was headed out of the plane.

I remember that moment vividly because of what followed.

THERE WERE SEVEN thousand people outside the Albuquerque Convention Center waiting for him in the New Mexico heat. There were another nine thousand inside. It was the first event I had attended as a surrogate for the Donald J. Trump for President campaign. Although I was aware of the national phenomenon Donald Trump's campaign had become, this was the first time I saw it up close and personal.

Albuquerque

The crowd in the parking lot exuded an energy like fans waiting to enter a rock concert or a playoff football game. As we drove in the SUVs through the throng, we passed young families, elderly couples, and everything in between, a sea of red MAGA hats. They waved, pointed, and shouted at us as we passed.

When we got out of the SUVs, the candidate and his entourage headed into the center accompanied by state troopers and Secret Service.

I lagged behind to look again at the crowd and take in the scene. It might have been that moment when I decided I needed to find out for myself. I'd been aware of the Trump rally phenomenon long before I'd joined his campaign—anyone who hadn't been aware had to be under a rock somewhere (or in Hillary Clinton's campaign)—but I still didn't know why it was happening.

I ducked around the Secret Service security perimeter and into the throng. As you might have guessed by now, I'm not exactly a shrinking violet. I walked up to people, introduced myself, and asked why they'd come. I'd known Mr. Trump for a couple of decades. I understood why people were drawn to him—there's a reason he was a star for all those years on television. It was more than star power or celebrity worship, however, that drew these people.

For the first time, I was seeing the true power of populism—what it means to people, and how it can be a refuge when no one else seems to be paying attention. But I was also worried. I had read enough history to know that movements such as the one Donald Trump was now leading often descended into chaos or irrelevance. By the time they pick up enough steam to effect real social change, most populist revolts become too unruly or watered down to be of any real use. This is the fate that befell the populist party of the early twentieth century, famously led by William Jennings Bryan, the antibank revolts of Huey Long, and the railing against intellectual elitism of men like Father Charles Coughlin. They're movements that are antiestablishment by nature, which means they have a predetermined shelf life in the United States of America, a country governed by money and establishment politicians.

The problem with most of these movements in general, and with guys like Huey Long and William Jennings Bryan in particular, is that they take aim at the elites, and then don't stop firing until they're out of ammo. They make bankers, entrepreneurs—really anyone who makes a few bucks—the enemy, and seek to divest those people of that wealth for the good of the lower classes. This message of redistribution and takeover by the masses can be appealing when you're in trouble, but it's nothing that can be sustained. It's not unlike what Bernie Sanders was proposing we do, probably that very day, a few states away from us. Populists are famous for appealing to resentment and anger but not proposing any solutions. If you want an example, go watch any clip of Bernie Sanders from any interview he did in 2015. If it doesn't have at least one of these words in it, "bank," "Wall Street," "*millionaires*" (emphasis Bernie's), I owe you a Coke.

William Jennings Bryan, who rallied people with his well-known Cross of Gold speech, about how the value of American currency shouldn't be based on gold, was no different. He once famously said, "No man who earns a million dollars could have come by it honestly." Huey Long, who founded the Share Our Wealth program during the Great Depression, often made the same mistake. He wanted a good life for everyone except those who were successful in business. They were doing well enough, he thought, and should support the rest of the people with the fruits of their labor. American history books are filled with characters like this—men who rail against the elites and hate anyone with money. They are good enough speakers to develop a devoted following, but their message crumbles the second they get within shouting distance of the White House or a city hall. No one—least of all Bernie Sanders, the only other candidate who connected with people in 2016—had ever been able to fuse the anger of the middle and lower classes with the power and money of the establishment and be able to lead them both.

When I began asking people in Albuquerque why they supported Trump, their answers made me start to believe that Donald Trump might be the one who could. Not only did those who came to see him not hate people with millions of dollars, but Trump's success in business was the main reason they were voting for him! They were angry with elites, with Washington, and with the people who'd negotiated all the deals that sent their jobs overseas. They knew they needed someone in their corner who understood the ruling elite and could battle it from the inside—someone who could fight for them and say things no one else would.

The people in Albuquerque were fed up. They no longer had any say in their government or with the people who controlled it. Years of systemic ignorance and government overreach had taken that from them. They had seen their communities begin to disappear, and their ways of life change dramatically. Some had been fired from their jobs and had no expectation of being hired again; others were saddled with massive debt, and had watched as the true value of their income declined with each passing year. For years, no one had been speaking for them or listening to them, including me.

I come from hardworking people, and from a neighborhood that once made anything seem possible. I've done pretty well in my life, and know a thing or two about business and the economy. Right under my nose, however, things had changed. Maybe I was too wrapped up in my high-octane success to notice that my neighborhood had gone from one of aspiration to one of desperation.

So, too, had neighborhoods in hundreds of other places such as Scranton, Beaumont, and Albuquerque.

Trump, the Blue-Collar President

I N NEW MEXICO, they spoke with a slight accent, at least to the ears of a guy from Long Island. They were a little softer on the vowels and quicker with consonants than people from Port Washington. But the words and the feelings were the same. These were the members of the aspirational working class, the ones I'd forgotten in my pursuit of wealth and success. They labored under the same dream that made my father get up every morning and drive his beat-up Chevy to the sandpits, the same one that lingered in the back of my mother's head as she stretched five days of food into square meals for seven days. It had been in my head, too, when I was placing newspapers on front stoops, delivering pizzas for tips, sinking my last few dollars into a new company. For the first time in a long time, I saw real evidence that the state of the American Dream was not well.

As I said, it took the campaign of a guy who lived in a tower on Fifth Avenue next to Tiffany to show me what was happening in America's middle class.

A little over six months later, Donald Trump would stun the world, his election whipping up a storm of resentment and controversy. The beginning years of his presidency would be as disruptive as any in the history of our country. Despite the maelstrom that surrounded him, not for one minute did he forget the promises he made to the crowd in Albuquerque or to the people in hundreds of other cities and towns he visited. Not for one minute did he forget the American steelworkers and coal miners. Not for a minute did he forget the construction worker and small-business owner.

Not for one minute did he forget the men and women who toil every day for a better life for themselves and their families.

In every negotiation, every executive order, every meeting he's convened, he has the American worker in mind.

His efforts have already paid off handsomely. As of the writing of this book, the unemployment rate for African Americans is the lowest it's ever been. The rate for women seeking employment, too, has reached historically low levels. Overall, unemployment has dipped below 4 percent, a number not seen in decades. Pay raises are the highest since the Great Recession. In the second quarter of 2018, the economy grew at an astounding 4 percent, and the president has announced he won't be happy until the GDP number climbs to 6. I don't doubt he'll help us get there. Manufacturing has come roaring back, adding job numbers each month that even surprise economists. With an unrivaled tax cut, folks have more disposable income. The summer of 2018 saw more people take vacations than ever before. Consumer confidence is the highest it's been in decades. Once dependent on foreign oil, the United States now exports it. Coal production is up for the first time in years, and the industry is actually adding jobs. The president has rolled back regulation after regulation that had handcuffed the American worker.

The stock market has gained as much as 27 percent under Trump, which has increased retirement funds and allowed many in a graying population to rest easier.

Construction is booming.

It seems like America's business has been hoping forever for a business-friendly president. We should have been hoping for a president who is a businessperson instead.

Still, the most important contribution Donald Trump has given the American worker is even more valuable than the extra money in their pockets. It's the sense of pride that has been restored. I can remember the look on my father's face after he came home from work, sitting at the head of the kitchen table, his work clothes still soiled but his hands clean. Though his home was humble, it was his castle, one that he worked his fingers to the bone to achieve. I don't think he would have been any more satisfied had he lived in Trump's triplex.

All across America, that same look has returned to the faces of men and women who are again making our workforce the greatest in the history of the world.

★ ✶ ★ ✶ ★

THE CANDIDATE WAS on his second bullet point on his folded-up piece of paper by the time I walked into the arena. He talked about all the towns he'd been visiting and what trouble they were in after the disastrous trade policies of the Clinton, Bush, and Obama administrations. He had just been in New York, and he spoke of our home state. He mentioned cities like Rome, in upstate New York, and towns not too far from Port Washington on Long Island, such as Bethpage and Hicksville. But he might as well have been talking about Clovis and Carlsbad, New Mexico.

Mr. Trump and I had been talking about NAFTA for a few weeks. As usual, he had also been discussing it with just about everyone he had come across. I was never sure whether I was telling him things he already knew, so I stuck to the basics. I also knew that he often used our conversations to find phrases that might resonate with people. We discussed how NAFTA caused the loss of sixty-five thousand factories in the United States between 1993, when it was enacted, and 2017. We made sure to keep in mind all the dumped steel that the United States was forced to accept from Korea as a result of similar agreements, and the hard toll that all that cheaply made steel had on places like Pittsburgh, Pennsylvania, and Youngstown, Ohio. These trade agreements with other countries, he knew, helped create the rust belt. They hollowed out the American middle class in the name of global prosperity—and the time had come to start standing up for ourselves again. Of course, I couldn't say that to a few thousand people and make it resonate. Donald Trump could.

"NAFTA has stripped companies out of your state," he said. "Stripped them out of other states…jobs down 50 percent, manufacturing down 50 to 60 percent. All these companies. Lost to China. Devaluation. They've treated us like a bunch of dumb babies, folks! Dumb babies!"

The crowd ate it up.

A S I WATCHED the end of candidate Trump's speech in New Mexico, I understood that I had signed on to something special. I was convinced that he had a real shot at winning the election, and that I wanted to be a part of his administration when he did. It also struck me, looking out over the crowd, that as much as I identified with the people in it—as much as they reminded me of where I came from and the people I still love today—I couldn't call myself one of them anymore. To borrow a phrase from the writer Thomas Wolfe, I couldn't go home again. I could only do the best I could with what I had, which at that time was a long list on my Rolodex of Republican donors, an understanding of how to craft narratives for candidates, and a sudden desire to do right by the people who had raised me and allowed me to become the person I am today.

I had already known that Donald Trump's populist movement would need institutional stiffs and big checks if he wanted to make it to the White House. He had recognized the need for someone like me—who'd savaged him on television and worked against him with two other candidates for months—long before I did, and he'd allowed me to come along for the ride. As I said, he's always ten steps ahead. If you're lucky, he doesn't hold that against you.

What the people in Albuquerque knew before I did was that Donald J. Trump would avoid the fate of the famous populists of the past. They didn't resent that he was the richest and most powerful guy around; on the contrary, they loved it. They loved it because they knew he hadn't forgotten the America that their parents and grandparents held dear, the time and place Fred Trump and Alexander Scaramucci came from. One dug the sand for the concrete, the other poured it into foundations, and, together, they built the American Dream. What the crowd in Albuquerque, and crowds around the country, believed was that Donald Trump would bring that glorious time back to us. He was their billionaire blue-collar president.

CHAPTER FIFTEEN

ELECTION NIGHT

"As I've said from the beginning, ours was not a campaign, but rather an incredible and great movement made up of millions of hard-working men and women who love their country and want a better, brighter future for themselves and for their families."

From President-elect DONALD J. TRUMP'S victory speech, November 9, 2016

E ARLY ON ELECTION night 2016, I sat in the Hunt & Fish Club with my wife, Deidre, and Steven Mnuchin's fiancée, Louise Linton, having dinner. It wasn't a celebration. Early polling did not look good at all for Mr. Trump. It's not like we had given up. Too many of our side's votes had yet to be counted, but when you consider that every major election predictor had Secretary Clinton winning in a walk it was hard to keep those thoughts out of your head. Louise, however, wasn't about to go negative. "Don't believe the polls," she said. "Steven saw other polls that were more optimistic."

I wanted to believe her, but an hour or so earlier I was at Fox News with other Fox anchors (I was anchoring *Wall Street Week* on the Fox Business channel) for a meeting with the Fox decision desk. They presented a memo that said that the exit polling was decidedly bad for candidate Trump in Florida, and he was likely to lose the state, and because of that, Secretary Clinton would be the forty-fifth president.

I excused myself from dinner early because I had been asked to speak at an event: Election Night Live at the New York Times Building. When I left my restaurant and began walking the streets of Manhattan toward Forty-First Street and the Times Building, the reality of the situation settled in.

When you've worked on a campaign for several months, election night can be a strange experience. For the most part, the work is done. The actions that move voters have all been taken, for better or worse, and the message is about as *out there* as it's going to get. All that's left to do, usually, is kill time and wait for the results to come in. For many of us on the Trump campaign, this was a little like watching a punch come at your face in slow motion. We were only about a month removed from the *Access Hollywood* tape, and the shadow of that news cycle was still long and dark. The Clinton campaign, on the other hand, was ready to pop champagne. They'd rented out the entire Javits Center for a victory party. Everyone gathered there—from journalists and political operatives to donors and private citizens—was expecting a massacre.

Still, visions of the campaign and the excitement that surrounded it started coming back to me, and I remembered why I had gotten on the Trump Train.

BACKSTAGE AT THE Times Center, I felt like one of those poor, disheveled Romans they used to send out to "fight" with the lions in the Colosseum. The seats were packed with three hundred or so writers and readers from the *Times*, who, judging by their applause for the speakers before me, were about 100 percent Hillary Clinton supporters. If they could have gotten tickets, they would almost certainly have been across town sipping champagne at the Javits Center. I imagined they wanted nothing more than to see Donald Trump go down in flames, then to watch him grab me by the ankle and drag me down with him. This was what comedians would call a "tough room."

I took the stage at eight o'clock and sat down in the dark with Nick Confessore, the journalist who was going to interview me. I like Nick, and thought he'd be fair. We sat quietly onstage for a moment, listening to the clicking and murmuring of the audience that sounded like crickets on a summer night. People were checking Twitter and texting friends for updates. Behind us were projections of those two Vote-O-Matic needles that had been running on the *Times*'s website all night. The needle on Donald Trump's meter was deep in the red, leaning heavily to the left, like the gas gauge of my old Camaro—the data folks at the *Times* gave him a 12 percent chance of victory. I had my own Vote-O-Matic in my head, however, and that still had Donald Trump with a 20 or 30 percent chance of coming out on top that night.

It was about eight o'clock in the evening when the lights came up onstage. Nick began the interview with a slight tone of pity, which he kept up for most of the half-hour session, speaking as if he were already in the loser's locker room asking what went wrong. I was careful to remind him it wasn't over yet, but conceded in a few places that the night would probably end the way he and everyone in the amphitheater were expecting it to end. Most of our conversation was affable and enlightening; even the audience seemed satisfied after the first few minutes. I was careful to keep in mind what I had learned about the camera, which was watching from the stage and recording everything we said: it likes authenticity.

Near the end of the conversation, Nick asked me how the Republican Party should rebuild itself after Trump lost the election—he phrased the question with *if*, but it was clear that he meant *when*. That irked me, but I didn't say so. I responded by talking about what I had seen during the campaign: all the families whose purchasing power had decreased sharply, the people who could no longer afford basic goods, the folks at the border who'd expressed valid concerns about rampant illegal immigration. I didn't say it at the time, but in those few minutes, I was actually talking about all the people that the reporters at the *New York Times* had failed for years to talk

to. I didn't think it would help anything to point out that they—
the writers and reporters in that amphitheater—deserved as much
credit for the rise of Donald J. Trump as any of the other forces I've
described in this book. It was the press who had ignored middle
America, and by doing so had pissed off, emboldened, and solidified
a political electorate that swept Trump to victory. The *Times* admit-
ted as much in an apology the newspaper published on its front page
after the election.

As I sat across from Nick, however, the chance of a Trump victory
was still remote. I ended our conversation by saying this, which I
still believe: "If the Republican Party does not open the tent to more
people and become more socially inclusive, then we are in grave
danger of becoming a minority party . . . I want someone who understands the economic principles that the Republicans are espousing,
but also has the compassion necessary to recognize where the world
is today, and where the culture is today." Looking back, it's funny to
think about the vision I had for the Republican Party—reeling from
a Trump loss, trying to convince voters to support sensible fiscal policies in the wake of the inevitable tax hikes that would have come
from a Clinton regime. Those problems seem far away now, more a
bad dream than anything that'll actually end up happening.

Today, however, we do have a Republican Party that remains
sharply divided over the leadership of Donald J. Trump and a whole
group of Democrats who are making plans to expel him from office
at the first sign of a slight electoral advantage. As a party, the Republicans have failed to include large segments of the population in
their decisions, and they continue to shut them out on key issues.
I believed then, and I still believe today, that our politics should
be less about left and right and more about right and wrong. Had
we ended up with a President Hillary Clinton—or a President Ted
Cruz or Jeb Bush—that dream would be further out of reach than

it's ever been. Those people were in the tank for the Republican and Democratic Parties. They would have deepened the partisan trenches and shut out everyone on the other side. Believe it or not, Donald Trump is our best chance at getting rid of partisan polarization in the United States. The Republican Party answers to him, not the other way around. He's also more open to new ideas and good arguments than anyone I've ever met. There has never been a president of the United States who cares less about left and right than Donald Trump. He also cares deeply about including all Americans in his vision for the country. I know because he's told me and despite the media's rhetoric, he deserves the chance to prove this.

THE INTERVIEW ENDED around nine o'clock in the evening, at which point I made a quick exit and found myself again on the streets of Manhattan alone. It was cool and busy in town that night. Traffic was moving quickly, and the poll results were flashing all over any surface with an LCD screen. If I had any thoughts about the election, I don't remember what they were. I walked the few blocks to the Hilton, happy the hard work was over for the night.

Looking back, I probably should have enjoyed my anonymity a bit more—the ability to walk down a street and have no one recognize me or care who I was. As Barack Obama, who's become well acquainted with this kind of fame over the last decade, put it, "once that anonymity is gone, you never get it back." But I wasn't thinking about any of that on my way to the Hilton that night. I was looking forward to maybe having a drink, maybe an appetizer, and a long break after a hard-fought campaign. I arrived, however, to a different story.

I walked onto the second floor of the Hilton to find the place alive with murmurs and speculation. People were saying that some of the returns from the Carolinas were looking good and that something interesting was about to happen in Florida. All throughout the second floor—which, in a show of our humility, wasn't even a ballroom, just a series of linked conference rooms we had turned into a large cocktail party for the night—people were much more optimistic than I'd expected. Walking around the room, I saw familiar faces from the campaign: Wilbur Ross, Ray Washburne, Mnuchin, Georgette Mosbacher, all of whom remain strong supporters of the president.

They were all smiling.

Around ten thirty, I sat down on the couch beside Rudy Giuliani, who'd been on the phone most of the night, monitoring the poll results closely while everyone else was chatting. He leaned in close so he could be heard over the noise of the room, which was increasing steadily as the party went on. "There are precincts that haven't reported yet in Florida," he said. "These are white-collar precincts. People there typically vote later at night, and they're going to vote for Trump."

From there, it was a blur. I watched as the big LCD screens played out Rudy's prediction in real time, and felt the room come alive around me. Where there had been sullen conversation and murmuring, there was now uproarious laughter and cheering. People threw their Make America Great Again hats in the air, hugging and calling friends with the good news. I don't remember how I finally found out Trump had won or what time it was when they announced, but I do remember how shocked all the anchors looked on television. It was as if they'd gotten the hard punch to the face we'd been bracing for all night. *About time*, I thought. Sometime around midnight I called Donald Trump's cell phone, walking over to a corner to avoid the noise. He picked up right away.

"Anthony," he said. "How's it going down there?"

Election Night

Mr. Trump had gone upstairs to his penthouse hours before, not wanting to jinx anything by waiting up in the campaign office. He sounded as calm as I'd ever heard him.

"It's going great," I told him. "Listen, I know you're working on the victory speech. You should put some stuff in there for the market. People will want to hear that."

Futures were down temporarily on election night, and no one was sure if they'd rally. Guys like Paul Krugman of the *New York Times*, who'd been writing for months that the markets would "never recover" from a Trump victory, had made people fearful about the election's potential effects on Wall Street. I thought Trump should get out ahead of that as soon as he could, which he did.

"All right, Anthony," he said. "We will."

After he hung up the phone, Trump moved to the dining room table in his Trump Tower triplex and started working on his victory speech. He'd instructed the team not to write a single word before he knew the outcome of the election, mostly out of superstition and fear of bad karma. Then he, along with Ivanka and Jared Kushner, would write a draft of his victory speech that included inspirational messages and an olive branch to all the people who didn't vote for him. It was a section of the speech, I've heard, that was presidential and compassionate all at once—closer to the real Donald Trump than anything he'd said up to that point. But that call to action would be attenuated, then nearly stripped from the speech altogether by some of the darker forces on the Trump campaign, who were also in the room that night. I would learn much later from people in the room that as soon as Ivanka added a line about being the president of "all Americans" to her father's victory speech, the man who would become President Trump's chief strategist would try to cut it out and add some half-baked lines about "enemies of America" and "American carnage."

Luckily, Bannon didn't succeed and instead the president-elect was his most gracious self.

This was the beginning of a very ugly fight, one that would become prominent in the early months of the Trump White House. On one side were establishment Republicans, who wanted to "protect the country" from the man the voters had just elected; on the other side was the Far Right, who sought to insert their own wacky ideas about globalist cucks and hatred for the press and the establishment into speeches and policy. Often, two-sided struggles like this one can lead to good things. Our country was founded on one, between Federalists and anti-Federalists, and it thrives on the basis of another, between liberals and conservatives.

This one, however, was toxic because it included toxic men with a need to satisfy their egos. It would be months before Donald Trump would recognize this struggle and begin to tamp down its negative effects.

Writing this today, it's easy to give the impression that I saw this struggle coming all along. But I didn't. Nor did I know that I would find myself right in the middle of the tumult. Back then I counted just about everyone I worked with on the campaign as a friend, and I carried that belief right into the transition. The transition, however, would become a breeding ground for creatures who would inhabit the Washington Swamp.

For the most part, however, my work during the transition involved vetting candidates for cabinet positions, coming up with cogent policy proposals, and planning out the administration's first few days in the Oval Office. I was involved in a few hiring decisions, and helped contribute to some of the executive orders that President Trump signed on his first days in office. One of the proudest moments of my life, however, came in the midst of all that grunt work and paper pushing. I was able to call my mother, who was probably at that moment framing a picture of her and Donald Trump, and invite her and my father to my swearing-in ceremony, which would be held at the White House on January 22. In a sense, this was my way of thanking them for all they'd done to help me succeed in life. It wouldn't be much, really—just a few minutes of ceremony and probably a tour of the White House, but to my parents, neither of whom had been able to go to college or do much other than work and care for their children, it was beyond their wildest dreams. It was also beyond mine.

I would learn quickly, however, that those wonderful feelings fade quickly in the Swamp.

CHAPTER SIXTEEN

WELCOME TO THE WHITE HOUSE

My one and only White House press briefing. (Chip Somodevilla / Getty Images)

WHEN MY COLLEAGUES in finance ask me what it was like working in Washington, DC, I tell them to imagine the worst, most maniacally ruthless person they ever worked with in business, Gordon Gekko with a genital rash, the kind of guy who would screw you over, burn your house down, rob you blind if it meant he would get ahead. That person, I tell them, would be an Eagle Scout in Washington, DC.

When an outsider arrives in Washington, say someone like me, they are met with glad hands and slaps on the back. The welcoming committee, however, has already swallowed two pills. One of them is an antifriendship pill. Dissolves under the tongue. Once you take it, it doesn't matter if you've been friends with someone for thirty years. If they think it might help them to take your eyeball out with an ice pick, they'll be Googling ice picks and sharpeners within the hour.

The second pill is what I like to call the power-as-an-aphrodisiac pill. It's like Viagra except that it stiffens your need to be important. Take this little blue pill and the most paramount thing in your life is proximity to the guy who's running the American government, arguably the most important person in the world. You're fighting over seats on Air Force One, worrying over the location of your office in the West Wing, counting every second you get to spend in the Oval

Office or talking to the man in charge. Anything it takes to get a piece of importance.

I know, I know. Sounds like I'm a little bitter, right? Maybe I am. Maybe they wouldn't really burn your house down. Maybe there aren't any antifriendship pills. I recognize now that the bitterness comes from my direct experience working with dishonest and unscrupulous people such as Priebus, Bannon, and Spicer. It may not be all of Washington; it just felt that way at the time.

E VEN THOSE FORTUNATE ones, the ones who can somehow sidestep the politics of personal destruction in Washington (the few, the proud), will tell you that the atmosphere in the town is like Beijing's on an overcast day. The place is toxic.

Don't get me wrong. Most of the people I met while working in Donald Trump's White House were good people with whom I got along very well, people like Kellyanne Conway; Gary Cohn, President Trump's chief economic advisor; Ivanka and Jared; Hope Hicks; Dan Scavino, the Twitter guy; Steven Mnuchin, Eli Miller; and the special assistant to the president, Johnny McEntee. All of the people who were with Donald Trump from the beginning considered it an honor to serve their country and were in it for the same reason as the president—to help the American people. Unfortunately, far too many people in Washington don't feel the same way. These are the Swamp monsters, or Swamp monsters in training, and they could care less about the American people. All these creatures care about is themselves, and they would take down anyone who got in the way of what they want.

Almost immediately after my arrival in Washington, two of them had me in their scaly sights.

Welcome to the White House

O N JANUARY 12, 2017, President Trump appointed me to head the Office of Public Liaison, the post that Valerie Jarrett held under President Obama. The OPL, as it's called, is like the networking arm of the White House. It's the office you go to when you've got interests you'd like to see reflected in policy. Not a bad gig, and I was perfect for the job. I knew business, what I thought business needed, and I'm a master at networking.

I had earned the appointment through my work on the 2016 Donald J. Trump for President campaign. I'd raised millions, gave $345,000 personally: $100,000 to the super PAC that Donald Trump Jr. was sponsoring, $100,000 to the inaugural, and $145,000 to Trump Victory, a joint fund-raising committee benefiting the Donald Trump campaign and the Republican National Committee. The reason it was an odd number is because I'd hosted—at my own personal expense—a breakfast for candidate Donald Trump in the Pierre Hotel in Manhattan two weeks after the *Access Hollywood* tape was released. The reason I'm telling you this is that Michael Wolff said that I had left the campaign after the tape was released and joined again when Donald Trump won the election. If he'd followed my Twitter feed, he'd have realized I was in full support of the president.

I'd also done countless hours of media advocacy for candidate Trump. I traveled to rallies, campaign stops, fund-raisers. I did all of this while keeping my hands on the wheel at SkyBridge Capital and hosting a weekly thirty-minute television show, *Wall Street Week*. Other than that, there wasn't a whole lot going on.

Priebus told me that I would have an office in the West Wing. Five days later, however, he changed his mind. Instead of the West Wing, he said, my office would be in the Eisenhower Executive Office Building, known as the old Executive Office Building. Built in the 1880s, the EEOB is a huge edifice that sits adjacent to the

White House. Lyndon Johnson ran the government from the building for a few months after John F. Kennedy was assassinated. The vice president has an office in the EEOB. To some, the EEOB is an exile. For them, proximity to power is power. If you're not within shouting distance of the Oval Office, you might as well be in Secaucus, New Jersey.

I didn't know enough to care. I wanted to be helpful to the president's economic agenda, and if they wanted me to do that out of a two-car garage, I was down with it. I'm a businessman. I could've run my hedge fund out of a phone booth, and didn't see any reason why I couldn't run the OPL the same way. Just give me a laptop and a cup of coffee, and send me on my way.

There were, however, a couple of loose ends to tie up before I started the new gig. First of all, there was the not-so-small matter of selling SkyBridge. I wanted to divest myself from my business so I could fully focus on serving the administration. That's all that mattered to me. I hired an investment bank to auction off my company. I received four bids and quickly reduced it to two viable buyers. One of the two was the HNA Group Co., Ltd., a Chinese conglomerate that had begun investing in the asset management field in the United States. HNA was actually the second-highest bidder, but I decided to go with them because the other buyer said they planned to fire half of my seventy-two employees. Going with HNA was a decision that would change my life, and not nearly in the way I thought my life was going to change.

IN THE EARLY days of the Trump White House, two words you would hear often were "globalism" and "nationalism." They were usually spoken or written in articles involving Steve Bannon, who'd made a career out of pitting what he called "globalist cucks," those who believe the world's economies and ideologies should interact, for example, the World Trade Organization and the United Nations, against people who care solely about America's interests regardless of how that impacts the rest of the world. To Bannon and others like him, it was either/or. You were either with us or against us. To anyone who's ever studied economics, this should have set off a few alarms. Weird internet language aside, the dichotomy is a false one, and historically, it has marked the beginning of some very ugly movements, particularly around the beginning of the Second World War.

Anyone who knows what they're talking about knows that globalism and nationalism need to exist in a symbiotic relationship. Individual economies need to be strong so that they can purchase goods made overseas by other strong economies. Without a healthy dose of protectionism from global competition, domestic economies can never be strong enough to keep the global marketplace moving. It's exactly the same principle that the US government had in mind when they enacted the Marshall Plan back in my grandfather's lifetime. When that plan was enacted, America was thriving and Europe was in big trouble. European countries didn't have the means to prop themselves up, so we helped them do it.

By the time Donald Trump came into office, however, the tables had turned. European economies had grown—thanks, in large part, to some massively unfair trade deals with the United States—and workers in the American middle class were the ones struggling. Luckily, we didn't need an international plan to help us recover. We could do it ourselves by "right-siding" some of the unfair trade deals and renegotiating with our allies. This is exactly what Donald Trump is doing at the time of this writing, by implementing a little tough love with our G7 partners. They've been allowed to pay slightly less than their fair share for too long, and it's time we did something about that.

Still, anyone who frames this as a war between globalists and nationalists is wrong, and I said as much at the beginning of the Trump presidency. It's much more nuanced than that, and I made it a point to say so whenever I could.

Over the Martin Luther King Jr. Day weekend, for instance, I flew to Davos, Switzerland, where I spoke at the World Economic Forum. (I had brought Klaus Schwab, the founder and executive chairman of the WEF, to meet President-Elect Trump a week or two before the inauguration.) In Switzerland, I told a group of world business leaders that Donald Trump was the last great hope for globalization. Thanks to inflammatory rhetoric by the Steve Bannon wing of the White House, my remarks were met with skepticism. I explained, however, that if you could create rising wages in America's dying middle class, you would create more purchasing power. More purchasing power begins a virtuous circle of consumption that will lead to global trade, and global trade will lead to more global peace, and more global prosperity. The virtuous circle is the foundation of Trump's economic vision, I told them, and my words played in Davos like music to the ears of some of the international business leaders in attendance. Back home in DC, however, not everyone in the new administration was clapping.

BY THE TIME I returned from Switzerland, Reince Priebus and Bannon had started popping those pills I mentioned earlier and began to concoct a plan to block me from the White House. Bannon saw me as a threat to his proximity to power and as an enemy of his phony agenda. He hated the World Economic Forum. He called it "the party of Davos" and said that the working men and women of the world were tired of being dictated to by international elitists. I'd gotten friendly with Bannon during the campaign and transition. I appreciated his grasp of history, helped him with his financial policy speeches for candidate Trump, and would often have philosophical talks about politics and the role of government. I didn't think we were that far apart in our views. Bannon, however, turned out to be one of the biggest hypocrites in a town lousy with them. He went to Harvard Business School; he worked for Goldman Sachs; he was a Hollywood producer—of some pretty weird movies, if you ask me— and then he went to work for the president of the United States. Can you get more establishment than that? He's about as antiestablishment as a Brooks Brothers suit with an American flag pin on the lapel.

As far as Priebus's problem with me? Well, for that you'll need a couch and Freudian psychiatrist.

I don't have a psych degree (I've played a therapist on *Dr. Phil*, though), but I have run two successful companies. From that experience I've learned a lot about human nature in a competitive environment. There's a type of person who works in the corporate setting who is so insecure, so lacking in confidence, so isolated, they become paranoid. Because of that paranoia, they feel that everything they have achieved is slipping or being taken away from them. They begin to develop trust issues with people who they perceive are more talented or more connected to others than they are. Petrified of losing their position, being labeled as stupid, or exposed as frauds, they develop a *Survivor*-like personality intent only on eliminating the competition. Simply put, they turn into rats. I'd been friendly with Priebus for six years. We'd worked together on Romney's campaign, and I even offered him a job at SkyBridge after the 2012 election. I'd kept in touch with him when he ran the RNC and was impressed with the fund-raising job he'd done for that organization. Then came the Trump campaign, however, and Reince began to change. Maybe his transformation came as a result of seeing Donald Trump bulldoze through the foundation of the Republican establishment he had worked so hard to secure. Maybe it came because Trump proved his core beliefs wrong. Whatever the reason, somewhere along the line, maybe sometime after telling candidate Trump to quit the race when the *Access Hollywood* tape came out, Reince sold himself out. He joined the rodent family in order to survive.

If you tried, you couldn't find two more ideologically opposed people than Bannon and Priebus. They formed their unholy alliance against me (and others) only because they needed to. To them, I was a wild card. Like the president, I was not entrenched in politics the way they were. I was a New Yorker, a successful businessman, and, most importantly, I had a twenty-year relationship with the newly elected president. They counted the length of their relationship with Donald Trump in months. Either one of them alone would never be able to move against me. Together, however, they thought they had a chance.

THE ASSAULT BEGAN predictably, a classic political hit job. They told the president, Kellyanne Conway, and others close to the president that a regulatory review revealed suspicious email traffic from my server to the Chinese conglomerate to which I was selling SkyBridge. Those emails, they said, showed that I used my influence with the president to inflate the price of my business. At the same time, negative articles about the deal between Sky-Bridge and HNA began to appear in Beltway publications and some major newspapers. I didn't understand—then—how the reporters got the details of the deal so quickly. To say I was politically naïve doesn't capture the situation. I was politically naïve to the twentieth power.

I hired Jamie Gorelick and Elliot Berke, two of Washington's best-known lawyers. Along with having the best lawyers in town, I also thought I had the best defense: I hadn't done anything wrong. No one would be able to find suspicious email traffic because none existed. Moreover, HNA agreed to the stipulations that there would be no contact with me during negotiations so that we could completely avoid any potential conflicts.

Under normal circumstances, the oppo move by Bannon and Priebus would have not only blocked me from the OPL job but might have blacklisted me for any position within the administration. Another president would have nixed my appointment just on the inference of impropriety. Reince and Steve's lie had become newspaper ink, "planted news" I call it, which is a cousin of "fake news." Planted news is a Washington operative's leaking of lies to sources to damage their opposition. They'll do this over and over again to build an oppo research file on the person they're attacking. That's planted news. And in another time, the planted news would have sealed my fate.

As it turned out, the planted news did work in the short run. I didn't get the OPL job. But they wanted me out of the White House forever, and that wouldn't happen, at least in the way that they planned it. They had underestimated my relationship with the president, whom I went to see shortly after.

"Why did you send emails to the Chinese?" the president asked me in the Oval Office.

"What are you talking about?" I asked. "I didn't send any emails to the Chinese."

"Priebus told me you did."

"Well, I didn't."

"Okay," he said.

That was that.

STILL, THE DOOR to the OPL had closed for me. Though that was bad enough, what was worse was the call I had to make after.

I'd never seen my mother as excited in her life when I told her she and my dad were invited to the swearing-in ceremony. She'd told all her friends. All her family. Everybody in the family knew they were going to the White House, and now they had to tell all those people they weren't. It was one of the hardest phone calls I've ever made. If Reince or Bannon had been in arm's length of me when I hung up with my mom I would have made them eat my cell phone.

The next time I spoke to Priebus, I told him that I knew he lied about the email nonsense related to HNA and that if he didn't find me a job in the administration things would get ugly between us. I was pissed, and he knew it. I might have been politically naïve, but I'm pretty sharp when it comes to the ways of the street. I know when someone is out to get me. On the street, if you don't kill the target, you've made yourself a pretty dedicated enemy. Reince had one in me.

The next thing I knew, he was offering me the post as the ambassador of the Organization of Economic Co-operation and Development (OECD) in Paris, France. Don't let the Paris part fool you. As far as Reince was concerned, it didn't matter if I was in France or with the penguins in Antarctica, just as long as I was far, far away.

Okay, truth be told, Antarctica and Paris aren't the same. Drinking good champagne and eating crepes isn't exactly freezing to death, and the ambassadorship would allow me to help the president interface with CEOs from around the world. It also could have been a stepping-stone to another position. But I didn't really want the job.

My mom has leukemia, and I wasn't going to be 3,500 miles away from her. The offer posed a real quandary. Luckily, I was able to buy some time. There were the usual background checks, a Senate confirmation, and the unusual review by the Committee on Foreign Investment in the United States (CFIUS) of SkyBridge/HNA. In other words, I wasn't going to Paris anytime soon.

Then, on June 19, while I waited for the OECD ambassadorship, Bannon and Priebus offered me a position at the Export-Import Bank (EXIM Bank) of the United States, the official export credit agency that lends to foreign companies to make US exports competitive. I know, I know. If you don't know what the bank does it sounds ridiculous, and, in fact, the president was thinking about shutting it down. The EXIM Bank, however, has been around since 1934 and has supported American jobs by facilitating US exports. I spent four weeks, from June 19 to July 20, as the chief strategy officer at the EXIM Bank, waiting for the all clear for the appointment at OECD.

Priebus and Bannon probably didn't spend a whole lot of time thinking about me at that point. As far as they were concerned, they had me shanghaied. They were just waiting for the ship to sail.

A funny thing happened on the way to Paris, however.

★ / ★ / ★

ON JUNE 22, CNN published a story on their website that accused me of having ties to a Russian investment fund that was under a Senate investigation. The story further claimed that the Treasury Department, at the request of two Democratic senators, was investigating me about a meeting I was supposed to have had with a Russian official with whom I'd promised to use my influence with the president to help get the sanctions against Russia lifted. (That influence was sure keeping me busy.)

There were three people responsible for the story: a longtime CNN editor, an editor who had won a Pulitzer Prize for the *New York Times*, and a reporter who had been a Pulitzer Prize finalist. CNN had lured that reporter from *USA Today* with the promise of being part of an elite investigative team. These guys were like a Navy SEAL team of journalists, which makes me wonder just how bad of a job the lesser angels of the press are doing covering this White House and those of us who orbit around it.

After the story broke, I went to see the president. I told him the piece was factually inaccurate and that they had used bad sourcing or, rather, a lousy source, because the story only used one source.

I also called an executive at CNN and informed him I was going to sue the network. I gave him phone numbers to the people in Treasury and in Senator Mitch McConnell's office who would confirm that I was not under investigation.

The next day, CNN took the story down and tweeted a retraction and an apology. I tweeted back that I accepted the apology. I've made mistakes based on hair-trigger decisions, so I knew what it was like. The network took it one step further, however. They fired the three journalists.

After the story came down, I went to visit the president in the Oval Office.

★ ✦ ★ ✦ ★

BEFORE I CONTINUE with this part of the story, it might be best to give you some idea of what the West Wing was like at this time. By June of 2017, the president's new administration was under siege by forces within that were trying to tear it apart by leaking information.

In July 2017, the chairman of the Committee on Homeland Security and Governmental Affairs, Senator Ron Johnson, published an astonishing report on leaks coming from the White House. An examination by the committee revealed anonymous White House sources leaking information to news organizations at the rate of seven times the rate of leaks during the Obama and George W. Bush administrations. Even John Brennan, Obama's CIA director, who is no friend of this president's, called the leaks "appalling." According to the report, information contained in the leaks included "intelligence community intercepts, FBI interviews and intelligence, grand jury subpoenas, and even the workings of a secret surveillance court."

The president was furious and frustrated, for good reason. His hands were tied primarily because of perception. He wanted to empty the place out, start over with a whole new staff. He was getting enormous pressure, however, from establishment Republicans to not make any rash moves. He also knew that the press would run out of ink writing stories about how his White House was in a tailspin. He needed someone on the outside to help him. And he needed it to be kept secret.

THAT SATURDAY, JUNE 24, I attended the wedding of Treasury Secretary Steven Mnuchin to Louise Linton, held at the historic Andrew W. Mellon Auditorium in Washington, DC. Vice President Mike Pence officiated, and the president and his wife, Melania, attended. The crowd at the wedding treated me like a conquering hero for taking down the big, bad, fake news, CNN. The president was especially happy.

A few weeks later, I got a call from Ivanka Trump asking if I would come in and talk to her and her dad. Ivanka and Jared are good friends of mine, and have remained so.

Ivanka's office is on the second floor of the West Wing. I avoided the White House registry or calendar, not wanting to draw attention or let any of the West Wing snakes know I was there. If either Reince or Bannon saw me climbing the stairs to the president's daughter's office, the West Wing's chapter of the deep state would have gone to DEFCON 4.

After a short discussion, Ivanka and I walked down to see the president, who was in his study, just off the Oval Office. The room where he sat has a seventy-inch television up on the wall. To him, it seemed that every few minutes something would flash across that seventy-inch screen that should never have gotten out—a memo, a conversation, some quote from an anonymous staffer about something way above their pay grade. Although the leaks had subsided somewhat in May and June, they had been nonstop for the prior months all the way back to his inauguration. The privacy of the West Wing is supposed to be sacrosanct, and there are good reasons for that. When leaked, meetings get taken out of context; ideas that are being floated in first-draft form get corrupted and distorted without the appropriate depth. Leaks pollute the process of governing—it's that simple. They cause a kind of paranoid paralysis.

The leaks were not only damaging his ability to run the country, they were hurting him personally. For some reason, loyalty has become a dirty word in the mainstream media. But dedication to people and ideals is what makes up the very fabric of this country; it's what made us successful; it's what won our wars and brings us the respect of the world. Donald Trump built a vast, successful international company, and if you asked him what the most essential element of his success was he'd answer with one word: loyalty. The leaks were an affront to one of his foundational beliefs.

I wouldn't blame you if you thought that the CNN story retraction served as the catalyst for my becoming the White House communications director. Without question, it did have some influence over the president's decision. In the Oval that day, he was again thrilled with how I had caught the cable news network red-handed. He was also disappointed with how his message was being presented to the public. He wasn't at all happy with Sean Spicer and the negative attention he was receiving from *Saturday Night Live*. Though Spicer was laughing about it, the president thought it was an embarrassment.

Timing is everything, and it certainly was for me that day. I was sitting in the den off the Oval Office in front of the president of the United States, at the confluence of two issues for which he needed immediate assistance.

It was at that precise moment when he decided to make me the White House communications director. Though he bestowed me with that official title, job one, the president told me, was to find and fire the leakers.

"You'll report directly to me," he said.

I'd like to think at that precise moment, somewhere in the West Wing, Priebus and Bannon were getting a bad feeling.

THE OFFICE OF the Chief Operations Services (OCOS) oversees the operational activities that maintain and run the physical, logistical, and security aspects of the Executive Office of the President, including the complex of offices and functions that support it. That night I had an event back in New York. When I turned my phone back on in LaGuardia Airport I had a half dozen new voicemails. Two of them were from reporters asking for a comment about my appointment. Someone in Operations must have tipped them off.

The other calls were from Reince and Bannon. I didn't return any of them. The next morning I flew back to DC and was having a cup of coffee at the Trump International Hotel. My phone rang, and I saw it was Bannon again.

This time I picked up.

"You have zero chance of being the White House communications director," he said. "Zero."

The guy had some set of stones. No "Hello." No "How ya doing?" No "How's the kids?" He goes right for the throat.

I told him I didn't realize the word "president" was in front of his name. Because if it were, I said, then my chances would be zero. But seeing how the guy who does have the word "president" in front of his name just gave me the job, I liked my chances.

Like Priebus, Steve Bannon had gone through a metamorphosis. He'd started to change during the transition. During the campaign, he was fun to work with. He's smart, extremely well read, and a great storyteller. But telling stories was his fundamental flaw. We used to say he had diarrhea of the mouth. For all of his antipress bluster, he loved talking to the reporters, giving them juicy bits here and there, always being sure that information made him look important. Leaking during the campaign is bad enough, but when your candidate has been elected the president of the United States leaking impacts national security. Without the regrettable language, what I said about Bannon in July of 2017 was true. The president repeated it almost exactly in a formal White House statement in January 2018 long after.

After the inauguration, Bannon began to feed the press on a daily basis and started to believe his own notices. The tale he was telling was megalomaniacal, in no small part because it suggested Donald Trump was his hand puppet. Do you think Joshua Green, writer of *Devil's Bargain*, came up with that little analogy on his own? It was as though he was borderline delusional, and I'm not saying that in the heat of some late-night phone call. His was a power-dream fantasy.

I told Bannon that I would meet him in forty-five minutes.

Welcome to the White House

In the White House chief of staff's corner office in the West Wing, Bannon was still coming at me hard. "Why are you going around our backs?" he said. "You don't know how to navigate what we're up against. You've never done this, blah, blah, blah." While Bannon was firing at me with both barrels, his face flushed, his eyes rheumy red, Reince was white as a ghost. He knew that once the president had named me comms director, he could start looking for a summer cabin in Wisconsin. They had only one hope, and it was a long shot. They needed to change the president's mind.

After about a half hour, the three of us headed down the hall to the Oval Office.

THE PRESIDENT SAT behind the Resolute desk, his jaw set and his eyes a steely blue. He looked from Reince to Bannon and then back to Reince again. You hang around Donald Trump long enough, you learn a couple of things. One of them is: sometimes it's just better to steer clear of him. This was one of those moments.

"You two are the biggest leakers I know," he said, before either of them could say a word.

The two of them stiffened. I'm sure it was the first time they heard that accusation coming from the president. Sarah Huckabee Sanders and Hope Hicks, who were in the room, wanted to look at anything except at the two bozos standing there dumbfounded. The president told Hope and Sarah to put out a press release announcing me as White House communications director and that I was reporting directly to him. He then looked back at Reince. The president's expression was one of absolute disgust.

"I don't want any of your taint on Anthony," he said.

It was war. Full on.

CHAPTER SEVENTEEN

THE CALL

In a press scrum on the White House lawn. (Chip Somodevilla / Getty Images)

On the president's plane. (Scaramucci family collection)

M ICHAEL WOLFF, the author of *Fire and Fury*, described
the West Wing as looking like the admissions office of a public university. I call his book "Liar and Furious" because Wolff is
a liar and Bannon, his main source, was always furious. Of all the
lies Wolff told in his book, his description of the West Wing might
have been the most disingenuous. Calling those hallowed halls an
admissions office is like calling the old Yankee Stadium a sandlot
or Babe Ruth a flash in the pan. The description ignores the history
contained by those walls.

One of my favorite places in the West Wing is the Roosevelt
Room, where I held meetings with the comms department. On
the walls there hang portraits of both Teddy Roosevelt and FDR.
They look down on you like centurions. The first time the president invited me into the Oval Office, I could feel my heart beating through my shirt. I imagined Reagan behind the Resolute desk,
JFK during the Cuban Missile Crisis, Nixon resigning. That day, I
asked the president what it felt like when he first sat there. He told
me it was thrilling, but that the biggest early moment for him actually came when he welcomed his first head of state to the White
House.

I think it was British prime minister Theresa May. He met her
at the North Portico, the White House's front door. As they walked

together down the hallway, he told me, the realization dawned on him: "Wow!" he thought. "I'm the president of the United States."

There are those who say that Donald Trump doesn't have reverence for the office he now holds. Nothing could be farther from the truth. He knows exactly the importance of the time and place he now inhabits.

OFFICIALLY, THE White House press briefing room is called the James S. Brady Press Briefing Room, and it's named after Ronald Reagan's press secretary, who was shot and paralyzed during an attempt on Reagan's life in 1981. The room is smaller than it looks on television. There are only seven rows with seven seats in each row. The order in which the reporters sit in the room is not haphazard. The White House Correspondents Association, the same club that throws the dinner every year where the president gets the chance to roast the people covering him from the dais (Donald Trump doesn't need a dinner or a dais to do that), controls the seating assignments.

The first row is reserved for the major networks and wire services, such as the Associated Press and Reuters. You might remember the woman with the long, sad face, Helen Thomas, who covered the White House for news services and other outlets going back to the Kennedy administration. She sat in this row. The second row is for the major newspaper and radio stations such as the *New York Times*, the *Washington Post*, and NPR. Large-city local papers, political blogs, cable news networks, and other media fill the rest of the seats. There are also "floaters" who have White House press credentials but belong to newer news organizations.

Interestingly, the briefing room is built over a swimming pool.

I'm not joking. The March of Dimes built it for FDR to exercise his withered legs. John Kennedy would swim in it with his Welsh terrier. It was President Nixon who created the pressroom, but he did so with explicit instructions to the workers not to disturb the pool in any way, in case a future president wanted it put back to use. In looking back, the pool serves as a pretty good metaphor for this point of the story, because I was about to take a dive into the deep end.

THOUGH FIRING THOSE responsible for the leaks was my job one, there was also the not-so-small matter of running the communications department. In looking back, I was naïve to think that I could just waltz in and do the job. But I also knew how dysfunctional the White House press department was, and I believed I knew the main reason why.

Steve Bannon had started a war with the media as a publicity gimmick. A lot has been written about Bannon's motives (in this book too). Some have said that his endgame was to take down the president. One thing is for sure, Bannon wasn't doing President Trump any favors by going onstage and calling the press "the opposition party."

Of course, it wasn't like the president was thrilled with the press either.

"I've had it with them," he said during one of our conversations.

I told him that he couldn't be at war with the media all the time, and I thought I could bring a measure of détente to the relationship, and maybe even start to till some of the scorched earth.

I knew it wasn't going to be easy. Nobody knows the press as well as the president. "The media used to love me," he said to me that first day. They did. Donald Trump has lived his whole adult life in the media spotlight. If you came of age in New York as I did, you felt like you knew him just from the front pages of the *New York Post* and *Daily News* alone.

"What the hell do you think happened, Anthony?" he asked.

"You let Bannon declare war on the media!" I said.

When the press turned on him, the president responded in kind, using his Twitter account like a heat-seeking missile against them.

"We gotta have an armistice with the media. You might not like them, they might not like you, but we have to stop battling each other," I told him.

It was then that the thought of the Lupus Foundation dinner, and the advice Donald Trump had given to me about handling bad press, came to mind. That thought was followed by the memory of Joe Margiotta and meeting Reagan in my senior year of high school.

I told the president the story.

"You have to let it roll off of you," I said. "Like water off a duck's ass."

He looked me straight in the eye. The president wasn't 100 percent on board, but I had gotten his attention.

"Okay," he said finally. "Let's fix this."

I was off and running.

I HAVE TO hand it to Reince. Right to the bitter end he tried every trick in his political oppo book to block my appointment, and hold on to his power. He had the press secretary's office issue a press release that said I wouldn't take over as White House communications director until August 15 to give me time to clear any entanglements with the sale of my business. Pretty cagey of him, right? The delay would not only give him over three weeks to talk the president out of hiring me, but the press release would lead to more planted news stories that made my deal sound fishy. President Trump, however, had already made up his mind. He directed me to hold a press conference that very afternoon. It was July 21, 2017. The White House counsel would make my appointment official later that day.

Immediately after the announcement, Sean Spicer resigned as press secretary, which worked out perfectly because he was one of the first people I was going to fire.

The next person on my checklist was Michael Short, who was Spicer's assistant. When I told the president that I was going to fire Short, he practically exploded.

"You mean he's still working here?" he said. "I told Priebus to fire him three months ago!" Short had been a critic of Mr. Trump during the campaign, one of many brought in by Reince. It makes you wonder why Priebus stuffed the White House staff with so many anti-Trumpers. Maybe he had his own endgame.

Spicer was another who had never really been loyal to Trump. The campaign had reached out to him for help when he was a strategist and communications director for the RNC, and he turned them down. At the direction of Priebus, Spicer undercut candidate Trump at the CNBC debate, something he must think that none of us remember. Perhaps he could have made up for his disloyalty during the campaign had he been any good at his job in the White House. His relationship with the press corps, however, was disastrous, not too far removed from Melissa McCarthy's hilarious impersonation that made him a laughingstock with the American people. Out of all of the missteps he made with the press, the most damaging might have been turning off the cross cameras in the briefing room. Those cameras are the ones that show the members of the press asking the questions. If you've seen a White House press conference, then you've seen the camera cut from questioners in the audience to the podium. Yes, the cameras play to the reporters' egos by raising their media profiles, but they also give the American people an intimate look into the open dialogue protected by the First Amendment.

Turning them off was a childish and spiteful move.

Things were just as lousy backstage. Spicer ran his press office like it was going to collapse at any moment. Everything was a tragedy; every bad piece of news was the one that was going to bring the administration down. Looking back, it's clear what was going on. He felt threatened, worried that he'd be found out as a B player. He had good reason to worry; calling him a B player was generous. What made his ineptitude even more obvious was the A player who would fill in for him.

A thirty-four-year-old mother of three and conservative Christian, Sarah Huckabee Sanders might have seemed like an unlikely fit for the briefing room podium. I didn't think so, and neither did the president. Sharp, witty (in an interview with George Stephanopoulos, she quoted LBJ: "If the president walked across the Potomac, the press would be reporting he couldn't swim"), and knowledgeable, with plenty of experience working for her dad, Governor Mike Huckabee, she had, I thought, all the tools to step right into the job. Still, when I told her the president was promoting her, she seemed shocked.

At that point, the press secretary's position in the White House was as hot as a pizza oven. From the first time she was behind the podium, Sarah was cool, calm, and collected. As a Roman Catholic, I've known people with faith and how they handle situations that baffle the heathens among us. Sarah reads a daily devotional. One of her favorite lines is "Come to me and rest. Give your mind a rest from its habitual judging." I think she should make copies and hand them out to the press corps.

JUST BEFORE MY only press conference, I met with the comms staff again, all thirty-five of them, in the press secretary's office. None of them knew me from a meatball hero. I was the new boss, however, and they began trying to get me up to speed with everything that they thought I needed to know, which was everything that was happening in the entire world: Syria, North Korea, Iraq, Iran—a crash course in about a hundred varied and challenging topics. I listened to about five minutes of the deluge.

"Whoa, whoa," I said. "Everybody, out!"

If I'd tried to remember even a fraction of what they were telling me, I'd have so much information flying around in my head I wouldn't be able to form a single sentence.

One thing I wasn't going to do was fake it. I was going to give them the full Mooch, and they could take it or leave it. As I said, the camera loves authenticity.

The same, however, can't be said about Washington, DC.

BEHIND THE PODIUM, and in front of the White House press corps and millions of American viewers, I answered every question as honestly and fully as I could. I will admit, I put something of a smoke screen up as far as my primary mission was concerned. Unlike those who were directing the subversive attacks toward me, I did not want to use the press or my position to hurt Reince, Bannon, or Spicer publicly. When the topic of media bias against the president came up, however, I told it like it was but also acknowledged the need to repair the White House's relationship with the press. And for thirty-five minutes or so, the relationship between the White House and the press was as healthy as it's been. Of course, that was before it was fed into our media's distortion machine.

Unlike the days when I placed *Newsday* on my neighbors' front porches, the news today is delivered in sound bites and five-second clips. So if you didn't watch my press conference live, all you saw on the news that night was me saying how much I loved the president and then me blowing a kiss to the room as I stepped from behind the podium. Right from my start, the press flattened me into a two-dimensional character—an Italian guy from Long Island, and everything negative that stereotype connotes.

There's a famous line that some people attribute to Give-'em-Hell Harry Truman that goes: "You want a friend in Washington, get a dog." I don't even trust the dogs there anymore. The town is like the writers from *Game of Thrones* joined the writers from *The Hunger Games* and *VEEP* to write an episode of *House of Cards*. It's not a matter of if you're going to get fucked in Washington; it's just a matter of when. For me, the countdown clock started to tick the moment Trump gave me the job.

Still, my job as White House communications director started off with a bang. I'm not taking credit for it. Sean Spicer had made the White House pressers into "must-see TV," and not in a good way.

Even without Sean's awkward surliness, however, the pressers' ratings would still be high. Anyone who thinks there is any other reason than Donald Trump for the revival in the news business is kidding themselves—someone with media appeal like his only comes along once in a lifetime or more. What people don't get about the president is how he handles the criticism. Does he get mad? Oh yeah, but he doesn't stay mad. Does he try to get even?

Yup, he can hold a grudge—what New Yorker can't? But people have this idea of him sitting up in the White House residence, rubbing his hands and plotting his revenge. Not the case. His skin is thick, perhaps the thickest of anybody's. On a strategic level, however, he is bothered when they say bad shit about him, so that's why he hits back twice as hard. It's not revenge for Donald Trump; it's business.

Afterward, I walked upstairs to the floor where the offices in the West Wing are. Sarah, walking beside me, looked at me in total bemusement. Though she would never say this, the words in her eyes were loud and clear. "You're a lunatic," they said, "but an entertaining one."

I told Sarah on the stairs that I had just done my first and last White House press conference.

"That's your job," I said.

I walked through the Oval alone and to the small adjacent study. The president was sitting there, remote in hand, watching his seventy-inch TV. He looked at me and then at the young naval steward in the room. The sailor looked like he had just walked off a recruitment poster. He was from Norfolk or Newport News, Virginia; I forget which.

"Tell him what you just told me," the president said to the steward.

"I said that this guy's going to help you, Mr. President," he said. "That was fantastic."

Then the young man shook my hand. It was an amazing moment, and one I'll remember all of my life.

The rest of my time as President Trump's comm director wasn't nearly as uplifting.

★ / ★ / ★

WASHINGTON, DC, not only specializes in the politics of personal destruction, it knows how to disseminate it. First, your adversaries paint you in a one- or two-dimensional way, after they flatten your personality, make you into a "Mooch is a mobster" type of thing, you're then fed like that to the rest of the world. No matter how intelligent or informed you are, the public can't help thinking of you in those negative terms. So when the Mooch talked, the public heard a mobster, because that thought had been planted in their heads.

On late-night TV, Stephen Colbert compared me to Joe Pesci in *Goodfellas*, Trevor Noah called my air kiss "the Mooch Smooch," and Seth Myers said I was a human pinky ring and a double-parked BMW. Okay, okay, the double-parked BMW is a funny line, but it felt like the comedians were mob baiting (so to speak), and TV was only the start of it.

Social media doesn't even have to try to deliver two-dimensional characters; it doesn't have the bandwidth for anything deeper. For instance, I'd send out a tweet, and two hundred, three hundred immediate replies paint me as a terrible person who left his wife, would screw over his investors, or, wait for it, just another guinea mobster like all successful Italian Americans.

I wasn't worried about Twitter—you grow a thick skin. Nor did I care about Colbert, Noah, or Myers. I can take a good joke. An Italian guy doesn't go naming his restaurant after John Gotti's favorite social club without having a sense of humor. It was Swamp creatures that I was worried about, the ones who smile at you and then reach around with their swampy claws and stab you in the back.

IT FELT AS if I was shot out of a cannon. The next couple of days went by in a blur. That night, I was hosting a party for my son at my restaurant, the Hunt & Fish Club. Along with eighty of his closest friends, Anthony Jr. had graduated the previous June from Manhasset High School. I wanted French Montana to perform at the party and had to wait for his schedule to open. If you don't know who French Montana is you're over twenty-five. His has six million followers on Instagram. Anthony Jr.'s life had also been rocked by my appointment. A Republican op I know had called him and instructed him to delete his YouTube channel because of threats against him on the site. In New York over that weekend, I did TV hits for Fox, MSNBC, CBS, CNN, and Breitbart, among others. You'll notice that this was an eclectic mix of news organizations, which was all part of the plan. I wanted to send the message that the communications office at the Trump White House was open for business, no matter which side of the aisle you were on. As far as I was concerned, everybody had a clean slate, and POTUS was on board with that. Can you imagine?

On Monday, I was back in DC. In the White House, I called the comms department in for another a meeting.

In their infancies, all organizations form competing factions, whether they're business, social, or governmental. It's just the way it goes. Depending on how much power, or perceived power, is at stake, those factions can become so disunited they dissolve into warring tribes. At the very least, they're susceptible to the fungus of negativity. Good managers realize this and put a stop to the dysfunction before it can cause lasting harm. I knew the culture in the West Wing was broken and the president was being undermined before I became comms director. I knew because the president had told me himself. I also knew because I had worked with most of the senior White House staff during the campaign and transition, when those factions began to form. Actually, some of the factions came to the Trump campaign team fully formed. There was the Republican

National Committee faction, those who were Washingtonian career operatives and who had some level of disbelief that Trump was the president. Then there were the leftovers from the Never Trump bloc, people who had concealed their disdain for the president and brought it into the White House with them. Though outnumbered by the others, there was also a vibrant Always Trump faction, those who were on the Trump Train from the beginning and happy to be part of the team. A gradation of all the different ideologies, the comms department was a microcosm of the entire West Wing, and was experiencing the same divisions and dysfunction.

So I knew there was work for me to do. I also knew that it was going to take time to complete that work.

The primary ingredient to a good meeting is dialogue, which I encouraged in the Roosevelt Room. I asked them to envision the optimal environment to work in. I told them to imagine having fun in their jobs. I asked them to start believing that we could work as one team. Now, I was under no illusion that the leaks would stop right away, and, in fact, a subsequent meeting with the staff was leaked. But in the confines of the Roosevelt Room that day, I thought I'd taken the first step in building camaraderie. Maybe I was just being overly optimistic. The putrid swamp of DC and most of the world at large, however, shared no such optimism.

On Monday afternoon, I flew on Air Force One to West Virginia with the president, who gave a speech to the Boy Scouts. On the way back, we ate Italian wedding soup. It was delicious. On Tuesday, there was a media day and I did dozens of interviews with news organizations spanning the media spectrum from Joe Piscopo to Wolf Blitzer. When's the last time you saw those two names in the same sentence? Later in the day, I had another meeting with the comms staff. By this time they thought I was a raving lunatic, but they'd begun to relax, which I was hoping to get them to do. Here's a baseball analogy. Though the New York Mets are my favorite team, I'm not a Yankees hater like some of the Mets fans I know. In fact, I've always respected the Yankees organization. They know how to put winners on the field. Maybe my favorite Yankees teams were the 1977/1978 vintage—the "Bronx Zoo" as reliever Sparky Lyle named them. There has never been a more ill-fitting group of guys sharing the same locker room. The manager, Billy Martin, couldn't stand Reggie Jackson, Jackson didn't like Thurman Munson, and Munson hated everyone. The Boss, George Steinbrenner, was constantly battling with Martin, and fired him—the first of five times—right in the middle of the 1978 season, and yet the Yankees won the World Series two years back-to-back.

Those Yankees, however, also had a lot of A-plus players. So my next move was to go scout out some A-plus players too. I wanted people who supported the agenda of the president, and who were smart, fast, and professional. I also wanted people who could get along with other people. You'd be amazed at how few of those types you come across in Washington media circles.

One of the first names to come to mind was Bill Shine. He'd been a pro for years at Fox News. He was always fair and seemed to never try to drive an agenda he didn't believe in. I arranged a dinner with him, Sean Hannity, and other Fox News personalities with the president and the first lady in the White House residence. I was hoping for it to be casual, just to get everybody talking to see how we all fit. As Donald Trump knows better than anyone, sometimes just hanging out, having a meal (or playing golf) is the best way to get business started.

The dinner went pretty much as expected. In spite of my intention, I found myself pushing pretty hard to get Shine to come work for us; I tend to get single-minded when I've got something in my sights. No positions, however, were offered or accepted that evening.

Which is why I was so surprised when I got that familiar *you're trending* feeling in my chest. For those of you who've had the feeling, you know what I'm talking about. If you haven't, the best thing to compare it to is the feeling you get when you think people are talking about you behind your back. Unless you're paranoid, which I'm not, it's like a Spidey sense, and accurate most of the time. That night was no exception.

Within minutes of our stepping into the residence, Ryan Lizza, the Washington correspondent for the *New Yorker*, tweeted about the dinner.

"Scoop: Trump is dining tonight w/Sean Hannity, Bill Shine (former Fox News executive), & Anthony Scaramucci, per 2 knowledgeable sources."

I don't know what your definition of "knowledgeable" is, but it's about the only word in that tweet that I take issue with. The rest was true. I did bring Bill Shine to a dinner in the White House residence, and Hannity was also there. If Lizza had called me, I might have given him the story myself. But he hadn't, and neither had any other reporter that night. I didn't tell anyone in the West Wing the dinner was scheduled either. It didn't take me long, however, to figure out how Lizza knew about it.

We had passed Reince Priebus on the way in. The leak could have only come from him.

The series of events that would follow that realization are not on my highlight reel. Unfortunately, I let my pride and ego get the best of me that night. The lesson I learned from the experience is worth sharing: when pride and ego are present, your decisions will likely be emotionally charged and muddled.

The Call

I made the call to Lizza as soon as we'd finished dinner. I asked him to tell me who leaked the story; in fact, I said that it was his patriotic duty to tell me. That was the first of many remarks I made on that phone call that I regret. I know that it's not a reporter's patriotic duty to reveal his sources, and I also know that it's probably anatomically impossible for Steve Bannon to do what I accused him of. And I certainly should have given myself time to cool down before I called him. Someone once told me that one of the smartest things you can do is pause. I should have paused.

As I said, I was politically naïve to the twentieth power. No other moment illustrates this better than my phone call to Ryan Lizza. The unwritten rule is that you verbally tell the reporter that what you're about to say is off the record. Although I hadn't said those exact words, we both knew they were implied. For one brief moment, a moment that would dramatically change the direction of my life, I allowed myself to believe that the conversation I was having that night was between two human beings, two Italian guys from Long Island, two guys whose fathers, Frank Lizza and Alexander Scaramucci, knew each other from the construction business on Long Island for decades. My sister, Susan, worked for Lizza's sister in a children's store. I thought there'd be a mutual respect there.

As I said, I was naïve.

Out of all the bad things I said on that phone call, the one that bothered me the most had nothing to do with Reince or Bannon. I'd told Lizza that I was going to fire the entire comms staff and start over. It was a stupid remark, and made in the heat of the moment. I would have never put thirty-five people out of work. If you don't believe me, ask the people who have worked for me at my hedge funds for twenty years.

For his part, Lizza wasn't nearly as emotional as I was during the

call, so I don't know what excuse he has for his callous reaction to my stupid statement.

"I laughed," he wrote, "not sure if he really believed that such a threat [of firing thirty-five people] would convince a journalist to reveal a source."

The irony is I wanted open dialogue with the press. I wanted Lizza and the rest of the White House press corps to feel like they could trust me, and that I could trust them. I've always believed that people need a little room to breathe—and curse and shout, if they feel like it—to do their best work.

At their root, however, writers like Ryan Lizza are in the gossip business, which is the fundamental flaw with the press covering this White House. Palace intrigue trumps (so to speak) anything of substance. So I guess I shouldn't have been surprised that he posted what I thought was a private conversation between two guys, one in which one of them was not at his best, for a few million people to consume. This wasn't Valerie Plame, it wasn't Deep Throat and Watergate, and it sure as hell wasn't the Cuban Missile Crisis. This was me ragging on Steve Bannon and Reince Priebus. But he went with the story anyway, and the story went viral.

I should note that he gave me a heads-up—of about two hours— before the piece was published and went viral. On the phone, he told me he'd written a story with whole batches of dialogue from me and that it'd be going live on the *New Yorker*'s website that evening. I think he expected me to be grateful. It was about then that the things I'd said started to flash in my mind.

Would the Bannon sucking his own cock thing be in there?

Why yes, Anthony, as a matter of fact it would be.

The paranoid schizophrenic thing about Reince?

You betcha.

The Call

You know what this story will do to me, right?
Oh yeah.

I N THAT MOMENT, my life became a car sliding down an icy hill sideways. I could turn the steering wheel as much as I wanted, but the car was going to go where the car wanted to go.

CHAPTER EIGHTEEN

EXPIRATION DATE

"Va Mooch! Axed after just 10 days"
New York Daily News
August 1, 2017

"Adios, Moochacho!"
New York Post
August 1, 2017

"The Mooch Takes a Fall of Biblical Proportions"
The Washington Post
July 31 2017

"Scaramucci Out: 'The Mooch' that Roared."
Fox News
July 31, 2017

"Kiss the Mooch Goodbye"
New York Amsterdam News

O N FRIDAY, July 29, President Trump named John F. Kelly, a four-star Marine general, as White House chief of staff. Though Reince had tendered his resignation a few days earlier, he got his pink slip from the president on Air Force One on a trip back from Long Island that same day. Although in hindsight it seems a bit ridiculous now, I thought I just might be able to keep my job. I spoke to the president on Saturday morning, and he told me to report to work on Monday. If I could make it to Monday, I thought, the news cycle, which moves at the speed of sound around the Trump White House, would have moved on. As it turned out, I didn't quite make it to Monday.

I flew home to Long Island on Saturday. The first indication came over the weekend when I called and asked for John Kelly's cell number and the White House didn't return my call. I flew back to Washington on the Delta shuttle early Monday morning. When I got off the plane, my cell phone rang. It was Nick Ayers, Vice President Pence's chief of staff.

"Why aren't you answering your White House phone?" he asked.

When I turned the encrypted phone on, I saw that it wasn't taking any emails. It had been deactivated.

At 8:00 a.m., I attended John Kelly's swearing-in ceremony as White House chief of staff. It was like going to my executioner's birthday party. At 9:37, he called me into his office. The ax fell quickly. He said that he was sorry, but that he had to let me go. He told me that he didn't think I would ever be able to get past the phone call with Ryan Lizza.

"Not in this town," he said.

I remember thinking that we had gotten past the *Access Hollywood* tape, but I didn't say that to him. Instead, I thought about how I would feel if I were in his position. As a business owner for thirty years, I know firing people is not an easy task; and this couldn't have been easy for him, especially considering it was his first day on the job.

"If you want to talk to the president about this, you're welcome to," he said.

I told him that wouldn't be necessary but asked if I could take care of a couple of things before I left. He said that would be fine, and I stood, shook his hand, and walked out the door. My White House career was over.

A career Marine, Kelly brought his military training and tradition into the West Wing with him. His mission was to restore order and the chain of command. He's received a lot of credit since taking over as White House chief of staff for his orderly approach and for plugging the leaks, and some of it is deserved. Some of it isn't. The truth is most of the major leakers had already been shown the door or were on their way out when he got there. Reince? Gone. Deputy Communications Director Michael Short? Gone. Sean Spicer? Gone, and, unfortunately for the cast of *Saturday Night Live*, probably not coming back. The only one who hadn't yet emptied the contents of his desk into a box was Sloppy Steve Bannon. (Kelly actually fired him the same day as me but gave him a softer two-week-later landing.) But he'd get his. In some ways, leakers are like drug addicts. You have to keep leaking bigger information and telling bigger lies to get your fix. Active leaking addiction never ends well. Bannon's sure didn't. Remember how he looked leaving the White House? A Harvard-educated cuck draped in contemporary hobo.

I'd also started to change the culture of leaking in the West Wing. Ironically, my firing was an example of that change. Kelly fired me at nine thirty in the morning, and the press didn't get the story until it was announced at two thirty in the afternoon.

One of the things I had to take care of in the White House my last day was to see the vice president. Though I had some official business to take care of with him, I also wanted to apologize. I was embarrassed that he heard the language I used in the phone call with Lizza. I'm only half joking when I tell you that I didn't think he'd heard those words before. Vice President Pence is one of the nicest human beings I've ever met. In a viper's nest like Washington, he's almost saintly. He couldn't have been more gracious to me.

I stayed in the Swamp for a couple of days. I had a room at the Trump Hotel and had dinner there Monday night. H. R. McMaster, the national security advisor, called. He had planned to host a party welcoming me to the West Wing the next evening.

"We can make it a farewell party," I said.

We laughed and made the plan. I went out to his house the next night, and we had a good time. Gary Cohn and some staff members joined the general's family. I even posed with my aviator sunglasses on for a photo with his daughters. About a week before I took the job at the White House I'd broken my sunglasses. I'd bought a new pair at the Oakley Store on Forty-Fourth Street in Manhattan near my restaurant. I thought they looked great on me. I was wearing them outside the White House one day (because it was sunny), and a woman came up to me and said, "You know those are women's sunglasses, right?"

I didn't know. I wouldn't have bought them if I did. But photos of me in the aviator sunglasses went viral: "Tony Goombah takes over the White House!" I did look a bit like a stereotype in them. The lesson is, don't ever wear ladies' sunglasses on the North Lawn of the White House unless, of course, you're a lady.

IT WASN'T UNTIL I went home on Wednesday that it all started to hit me. I felt pretty low. I'd gone from something of a financial celebrity who was a regular on cable finance channels like CNBC, Fox Business, and Bloomberg to being on the front page of major city newspapers from around the world. I went from having my own weekend show, *Wall Street Week*, with fifty thousand viewers, to a story so viral it nearly made the internet explode. Or so it seemed.

I'd asked in a tweet for the gossip media to stay out of my personal life, but that was like asking cockroaches to stay out of spilled milk. The editors of *Page Six* were especially intrusive and nasty. I know it's their stock-in-trade, but what I don't understand is how anybody could write hurtful things like they do and then look themselves in the mirror. My wife, Deidre, had filed for divorce when she was eight months pregnant. I'd been with the president in West Virginia at a Boy Scout jamboree when our son James was born three weeks early in New York. Deidre and I were fighting all the time. My wife believed that I had put my job at the White House ahead of her and our first son, Nicholas. I guess I had. I'd become involved in politics because, as a businessperson, I'd hoped I could someday be in a position to influence policy. I found myself in that position faster than I could have imagined—at the side of the president of the United States. When you're in the middle of a dream, it's hard to see anything or anyone else—even those you care about the most. I now take responsibility for my actions; I was wrong, but that didn't give the media the right to publicize my personal troubles for click-bait or to sell newspapers.

★ / ★ / ★

B Y WEDNESDAY EVENING, every journalist with a press card, every TV news producer, and every cable news host, it seemed, was calling me, looking for an interview. I felt trapped. When you're a story as viral as I was, there's no place to hide.

That night and the next day, I did a lot of soul-searching. I'm a grown man, with an Ivy League degree, and I'm a father of five children including a beautiful daughter; there was no reason for me to use that kind of language with anyone, in any circumstance, let alone talking to a reporter. In the whole scheme of things, though, how big of a deal was it?

What bothered me the most was the impact it had on my family. After my mother shooed the press away from her lawn, she said quietly to me, "Why'd you have to say those things?"

She'd been so proud. She had hung an eight-by-twelve photo (the one she looked the best in) of her with President Trump on the Scaramucci Wall of Fame. There was also a smaller one (the one in which she didn't like the way she looked) with her and my dad with the president. It wasn't only my parents I disappointed. There were my brother, uncles, cousins, and nephews and nieces. My sister, Susan, had taken a job as a travel agent. She was flying to Atlanta when I was fired. When she landed she had thirty voicemails and I was on every TV in the airport. One of the agents she met started to rant about what a horrible person I was. The agent didn't know that Susan was my sister. "He's my brother," my sister said to her, "and you have no idea what kind of a person he is."

The president called me that day to ask how I was doing, which made me feel better. Donald Trump is a considerate man. I also took the opportunity to tell him how I felt. The difference between my relationship with President Trump and many people in his orbit is that I've never been a sycophant. I've always told him and will always tell him exactly how I feel. The conversation I had with him that day was no different. I told him that I had spent two years working for him, donated a lot of money to his campaign, and did whatever I could to get him elected—including nearly ruining my marriage and business. So yes, I said, I felt a little slighted. I told him I didn't expect him to come riding to my rescue. I knew I'd put him in a position where he couldn't help me. But I still felt hurt, and I think it had less to do with why I was fired and more with the way I was fired and who fired me.

I told the president that I didn't think it was a wise idea to try to run a civilian organization like the West Wing as if it were the military. A four-star general's presence almost by definition creates some level of fear and anxiety. Bringing Kelly aboard wouldn't mollify the paranoia in the West Wing. If anything his presence would exacerbate it.

But more importantly, I said, the general's style would be in direct conflict with the way he had always conducted business.

President Trump doesn't work in a precise way. Never has. Never will. As I mentioned, one of his strengths is how easily he reads people, how he extracts and interprets information from them to inform his decisions. He needs people around him, people he knows and trusts. Keeping President Trump sealed off from that free flow of information is a travesty and a detriment to the administration and the president's policies.

It's been over a year since John Kelly became the White House chief of staff, but my scouting report early on proved to be quite accurate. His personal insecurity has proven to be a poor match with the self-confident, gregarious president. According to the press,

Trump's and Kelly's personality differences have now left Kelly disconnected from the process and ineffective in his job. Kelly has also been incapable of recruiting a compatible staff to work with him, so there's no one there to take up his slack. I'm hopeful that the president will choose someone as his next chief who actually likes him.

The conversation with President Trump was brief but heartfelt. I hung up knowing that our relationship would continue. Once you're a friend of Donald Trump like I was, you have to do more than just get fired to get kicked out of it. I'm proud to say I'm still the president's friend and proud to continue to help him keep America great.

I KNEW I wasn't going to have the White House job forever. I just thought I would have lasted longer than a quart of milk. I still wonder what would have happened if the president had given me another chance. I think I would have learned the comms director position and done a good job. (I might have learned more in eleven days than a lot of White House communications directors learn in their whole tenure.) Just like the Navy steward had said, I think I would have also helped the president, even more than I did. I still don't believe President Trump is doing himself any favors by continuing Steve Bannon's war with the press. I had put together a White House communications plan that I was ready to start executing the day I was fired. With time, I think I could have helped repair the relationship in the briefing room. I know there are men and women in that pressroom and beyond who are good, professional reporters just trying to do their jobs. Belittling them day in, day out has to affect the stories they choose to report and write. That's a shame because there are a lot of good stories coming from this White House that aren't getting the attention they deserve, including how the president's policies and agenda have helped blue-collar America.

★ / ★ / ★

B Y AUGUST 7, I knew I needed to get away. Not run away, but go someplace where I felt safe and far from all the toxicity.

My son AJ lives in Marina del Rey. I'd met his mother, my first wife, Lisa, on the campus at Tufts. We married early and stayed together for over two decades.

Alexander, whom we call AJ, is our oldest and was born in 1992. Three years later Amelia, our daughter, came along, and four years after that came Anthony Jr. I think about that time and being so young with a family and a growing career, and it reminds me of the Harry Chapin song "Cat's in the Cradle." I tried my hardest to be the best dad I could. I went to baseball games and recitals and took them every year to Disney World and the Mets training camp in Port St. Lucie, Florida. I made sure they all went to public schools. I didn't want them to grow up thinking they were privileged. Rich kids, I told them, are born on third base and tell everyone they hit a triple—at least some of them do. You have to take your own swings, I said.

Still, I spent far too much of their childhood in pursuit of the next level in business. Don't get me wrong. There is nothing wrong with striving for more, making success a priority, and becoming the best provider you can be. I'm proud of all that I accomplished in business. The price for what I obtained, however, was steep. I paid for my success with hours stolen from my family, with moments missed, and with memories that I buried to make room for things that I thought were more important but weren't.

Though mismatched, Lisa and I have three beautiful children. Lisa's a terrific mother and gets most of the credit for raising our kids to become wonderful young adults. I tried as hard as I could. I guess the proof of how well you raised any child is how they turn out.

After he graduated from college, AJ went to work for Google. He then became an entrepreneur in residence for Peter Diamandis, the best-selling author and entrepreneur specializing in space, longevity, and innovation. Diamandis founded the XPRIZE Foundation, which began by awarding money to spacecraft development and has morphed into awards for work in all kinds of categories, including adult literacy and artificial intelligence. All above my pay grade. AJ's now finishing up his postgraduate degree at the Stanford Graduate School of Business.

Like her dad, Amelia is more at home in front of the camera. A talented actor and singer, in 2012 she wanted to audition for the movie *Les Miserables*. I called Ed Pressman, the producer of *Wall Street: Money Never Sleeps*. He called the casting director. There's an old expression in Hollywood, however, that goes: You can only buy yourself to the middle. The rest of the way you have to rely on talent. Amelia crushed the audition and got the role. She went on to study drama at Brown University and has since appeared in several films.

Anthony Jr. is a Division I lacrosse player at Sacred Heart University in Connecticut. He wants to get into the film business, but behind the scenes. He's a talented screenwriter and has already made some rap video films.

I love all of my kids equally, but I knew where I would find my solace.

I booked a flight to California.

In Santa Monica, AJ and I walked on the Third Street Promenade looking for a place to eat. My son has been on his own for some time now, finishing school and with a burgeoning business career. Still, when I first saw him on that trip, I had to fight the urge to tousle his hair. It didn't seem so long ago that I would be holding his hand on a walk like the one we took. Ask any dad: when you look into your adult child's eyes, most of the time a six-year-old looks back at you. Dads will also tell you there comes a moment when that six-year-old disappears and a grown man takes his place.

Writing this makes me think about my own father. I'm not going to sugarcoat our relationship. My dad was not an easy guy to get along with. He had a temper that makes mine look like a nursery school teacher's. There was never a question in my mind, however, that he loved me. I remember my first year in college when the tuition bill came. In my memory, I can see him holding the piece of paper in his hand. How many hours of digging sand did that life insurance policy represent, I wonder.

"But, Dad," I'd said. "It's important you have that policy."

"It's more important that you go to school," he said as gently as I've ever heard him say anything. That's what America is supposed to be. A country in which sons and daughters stand on their parents' shoulders to reach as far to the sky as they can.

★ ✸ ★ ✸ ★

THROUGHOUT MY LIFE, I've come to realize that big emotional moments never come when you're expecting them. The guy who fires you ends up giving you a recommendation that gets you a better job. Your company is about to fail and the whole global economy is on the brink of collapse, but a short conversation with your brother is what makes you want to cry. You feel sorry for yourself when you get fired from the White House, but then you get hit with a big wave of love and gratitude on a simple walk with your son. Sometimes, this stuff just comes up out of nowhere.

The Promenade was relatively crowded, and several people recognized me. My life outside the White House had become considerably different from the one I had before I went to work for the president. It had changed forever. AJ told me that he had counted the negative news stories about my firing listed on Google. There had been 180. At one point on our walk, my son stopped and looked at me. Those handsome brown eyes filled with concern.

"You going to be all right, Dad?" he asked.

In that moment, the six-year-old disappeared, and a full-grown man took his place. My son was now taking care of me.

I'VE LIVED AN improbable life for an Italian kid from Webster Avenue in Port Washington whose father worked in the sandpits. I was lucky enough to go to some of the best schools in the country, I've made more money than I could have imagined, had businesses succeed and fail, thought life would never be the same after a beautiful September morning in 2001, lost and found love, and watched my five healthy and beautiful children grow.

I also had the privilege of working on a presidential campaign about which historians will write volumes, and for a candidate who changed politics forever. And, for eleven days, I worked in the White House for a president and an administration that I believe is changing America for the better. I put my arm around AJ's shoulder.

"We're going to be fine," I said to my son. "Better than fine."

CHAPTER NINETEEN

THE TWELFTH DAY

The Scaramucci family at my mom's 80th birthday celebration. (Scaramucci family collection)

My beautiful wife Deidre and our son Nicholas. (Scaramucci family collection)

This is the one hanging on the wood-paneled wall in my parent's house. Mom and the President. (Scaramucci family collection)

BELIEVE IT OR NOT, when F. Scott Fitzgerald first published *The Great Gatsby* in 1925, it didn't cause much of a stir. Reviews in the newspapers were mixed: some high-minded people enjoyed the story, but few people bought it. While his first two books, *This Side of Paradise* and *The Beautiful and Damned*, flew off the shelves, big stacks of his third novel gathered dust in the display cases. Panic set in. He got writer's block. On top of all that, he had to read articles every day about contemporaries like Ernest Hemingway and Thomas Wolfe who were writing up a storm and selling books by the truckload while he could hardly get a word out.

Fitzgerald died broke at forty-four from alcoholism, thinking *Gatsby* was a failure. In one of the last notebooks he ever kept, he wrote this: "There are no second acts in American life."

The line has been used in writing so many times it's a cliché. Not because there's any truth to it, but because there isn't. Had Fitzgerald put down the bottle and hung around long enough he would have found that out for himself. I read somewhere recently that the trade-paperback edition of Gatsby sells about a half million copies a year—nearly ninety years after the original was published.

When I first came up with the idea of writing this book I wanted to call it *The Twelfth Day*, and I wanted the theme to be about second acts. What I realized, however, is that the second act means nothing if you haven't learned from the first one.

I hope I have.

F. Scott Fitzgerald has another quote people use all the time. This one is a bit more on the mark: "The test of a first-rate intelligence is the ability to hold two opposing ideas in mind at the same time and still retain the ability to function." I would add, the test of a first-rate emotional intelligence is the ability to forgive yourself while keeping a sense of humor and an appreciation for what you have. Without question, I like what I have.

Deidre and I are back together and working on our relationship. There's too much love in our marriage to let it slip away. We even did a *Dr. Phil* show, and who knows, maybe we'll go back for a tune-up if we need to. We have two beautiful sons, Nicholas and James, whom I love with all my heart. If I've learned anything from my experience over the last few years, it's that life and family are more important than politics.

You might have read that I'm back at SkyBridge. The deal had been in front of the Committee on Foreign Investments in the United States (CFIUS), which reviews and approves transactions such as the one SkyBridge had with HNA. To be honest, the name of the committee, CFIUS, sounds like a venereal disease to me, but I don't want to give you the wrong idea. It's a heavyweight organization. Among those who sit on the CFIUS committee are the secretaries of state, defense, commerce, justice, and homeland security. The secretary of the treasury, Steven Mnuchin, is the chair of the committee. The SkyBridge/ HNA deal sat in front of the CFIUS committee for six months, and all indications were it wasn't going to be approved anytime soon. CFIUS hadn't approved the deal for a number of reasons, including the complicated relationship the United States now has with China. None of those reasons, however, had anything to do with the lies put forth by the Swamp creature who used to swim in the West Wing.

Management teams for both HNA and SkyBridge decided that we didn't want to wait any longer. My reaction to the news was a mix of relief, disappointment, and excitement. Selling the firm would have created a significant windfall, but that was not the source of my dissapointment. My disappointment was borne of the realization that I would not get the opportunity to work tirelessly on behalf of the American people. As I mentioned before, it would have been a dream come true to be given a chance to have a small say in how government and business interact.

On the other hand, I'm comfortable being back at SkyBridge, a company of which I am very proud. Being fired from the White House, while difficult, made me more appreciative of my former life. My management style is the same, but I'm a lot more grateful—for my family, for my friends, and for my business. I've been given a second act with SkyBridge, and I intend to take full advantage.

My friendship with the president has also entered its second act. I call myself an FBL, Fired but Loyal. (There's a growing number of us.) From my current vantage point, I might be in a better place to help the president than when I was on the inside. The way I look at it, I'm still in the orbit, but far enough away to have an objective view. This makes me a desirable guest on shows that don't often hear the Trump side of things.

The president needs people like me who can call balls and strikes and who will tell him the unvarnished truth about his policies and tactics, good and bad.

The Trump presidency is far from perfect. Some of the imperfections, however, are the result of a broken system. In this age of news saturation, elected officials stay in campaign mode throughout their terms of office, and that's a shame. Rhetoric that excites President Trump's base makes it hard for a large segment of the population to get behind him. But the Left is always campaigning too, which, by definition, does not allow compromise. Still, there comes a time to govern for all, not just for your voting base. I've told him that.

This might come as no surprise, but our president can be stubborn. When the Left throws a temper tantrum about a position he takes, he digs in. Believe me, I know that shouting at Donald Trump is not the way to get through to him. When he's not on the defensive, or fighting back, he might be the most flexible president to ever hold the office. I've seen him align with Bernie Sanders and Ted Cruz, all in the same week. Because of his flexibility, he's able to approach problems in an unorthodox way that can often cut through decades of protocol, red tape, and orthodoxy that other presidents have to navigate through before they even get to the problem; his negotiations with North Korea are a prime example. Lost in the sea of hysterical news ink about Russia and conspiracies is a set of decisions and policies that are driving our economy, making us safer, creating jobs, and returning us to the respected place in the world that we once occupied.

I believe we have a real opportunity in a Trump presidency to change things dramatically for the good. We might never have a president again who can move intractable barriers the way he does.

Maybe we can all learn something from President Trump's first act. If we can, then there's no limit to how great the second act can be.

Somewhere the theme from *Rocky* has started to play.

ACKNOWLEDGMENTS

First and foremost, I send all my love to my wife, Deidre, and my children: AJ, Amelia, Anthony, Nick, and James; to my parents, Alexander and Marie Scaramucci; and to my brother and sister, David and Susan.

I want to thank the free press for the gift they have given to our society. That gift not only holds our leaders accountable, it teaches our children to think independently. There are too many whom I respect to name here, but here are a few on my All-Star team: Sean Hannity, Jeanine Pirro, Bill Hemmer, Sandra Smith, Maria Bartiromo, Steve Doocy, Brian Kilmeade, Ainsley Earhardt, Peter Hegseth, Martha MacCallum, Jesse Watters, Chris Cuomo, Jake Tapper, Greg Gutfeld, Dana Perino, Alysin Camerota, John Berman, Don Lemon, Christie Bear, Jeff Zucker, Stephanie Ruhle, Katy Tur, Emily Maitlis, Ari Melber, Phil Griffin, Brian Karem, Governor Mike Huckabee, Maggie Haberman, Howard Bragman, Jennifer Connelly, Suzanne Scott, Brian Steel, Scott Wapner, and Mark Hoffman.

ACKNOWLEDGMENTS

A big shout-out goes to Tony and Sage Robbins, who were there for my wife, Deidre, and me when we needed them.

My love goes to my uncle Sal DeFeo and cousins Sonny, Bobby, and Augie DeFeo. A special thanks to my agent, Ian Kleinert, and to the team at Center Street: publisher Rolf Zettersten, my fabulous editor, Kate Hartson, Patsy Jones and her great marketing and publicity team, and Cheryl Smith and the Hachette Audio team. I want to thank Brian McDonald and Sean McGowan for their guidance and research, and I send my love to my closest friends: Bob Castrignano, Brett Messing, Bob Matza, Paul Montoya, and Todd Magazine. I want to thank the entire staff at SkyBridge, including my partners Ray Nolte, Marie Noble, Rob Phillips, Jason Wright, Robert Duggan, Chris Hutt, and Victor Oviedo.

Last but not at all least, I want to thank my friends in the Trump Administration. Given the current political environment, however, I thought it best not to name you. You know who you are, and I am grateful to you for your help and support.

ABOUT THE AUTHOR

ANTHONY SCARAMUCCI is the founder and co-managing partner of SkyBridge Capital. He is the author of three books: *The Little Book of Hedge Funds*, *Goodbye Gordon Gekko*, and *Hopping Over the Rabbit Hole*, a 2016 *Wall Street Journal* best-seller. Prior to founding SkyBridge in 2005, he co-founded the investment partnership Oscar Capital Management, which was sold to Neuberger Berman, LLC in 2001. Earlier, he was a vice president in Private Wealth Management at Goldman Sachs & Co. Anthony is a member of the Council on Foreign Relations (CFR), vice chair of the Kennedy Center Corporate Fund Board, a board member of both The Brain Tumor Foundation and Business Executives for National Security (BENS), and a Trustee of the United States Olympic & Paralympic Foundation. He was a member of the New York City Financial Services Advisory Committee from 2007 to 2012. He holds a Bachelor of Arts degree in Economics from Tufts University and a Juris Doctor from Harvard Law School.